William Howitt

Ruined Abbeys and Castles of Great Britain

William Howitt

Ruined Abbeys and Castles of Great Britain

ISBN/EAN: 9783744793629

Printed in Europe, USA, Canada, Australia, Japan

Cover: Foto ©ninafisch / pixelio.de

More available books at **www.hansebooks.com**

Ruined Abbeys and Castles

OF

Great Britain.

BY

WILLIAM AND MARY HOWITT.

The Photographic Illuſtrations

BY

BEDFORD, SEDGFIELD, WILSON, FENTON,

AND OTHERS.

London :
A. W. BENNETT, 5, BISHOPSGATE WITHOUT.

1862.

PREFACE.

In this volume the Publisher has availed himself of the accuracy of Photography to present to the reader the precise aspect of the places which, at the same time, are commended to his notice by the pen. It appears to us a decided advance in the department of Topography, thus to unite it to Photography. The reader is no longer left to suppose himself at the mercy of the imaginations, the caprices, or the deficiencies of artists, but to have before him the genuine presentment of the object under consideration. We trust that this idea of our Publisher will be pursued to the extent of which it is capable; and that hereafter we shall have works of topography and travel, illustrated by the photographer with all the yet-to-be improvements of the art, so that we shall be able to feel, when reading of new scenes and lands, that we are not amused with pleasant fictions, but presented with realities. With this sentiment we submit the present work to the public, as a step in the right direction, and as an evidence on the part of the publisher of a desire to assist in authenticating literature by the splendid achievements of modern art.

21*st October*, 1861.

CONTENTS.

	PAGE.
Bolton Priory	1
Glaſtonbury Abbey	13
Iona, or Icolmkill	37
Lanthony Abbey	52
Chepſtow Caſtle	61
Tintern Abbey	74
Raglan Caſtle	87
Conway and its Caſtle	96
Goodrich Caſtle and Court	123
Fountains Abbey	138
Roſlin Chapel and Caſtle	148
Elgin Cathedral	161
Holyrood Abbey and Palace	167
Melroſe Abbey	179
Cariſbrooke Caſtle	192
Rievaux Abbey	203
Furneſs Abbey	215

Illustrations.

		PAGE.
Bolton Priory	By W. R. SEDGFIELD	4
——; *The Strid*	,, DO.	9
Glastonbury Abbey; Chantry Chapel	,, DO.	25
Iona	,, G. W. WILSON.	40
Lanthony Abbey	,, F. BEDFORD.	53
Chepstow Castle	,, DO.	65
——; *Marten's Tower*	,, DO.	71
Tintern; view from Chapel Hill	,, W. R. SEDGFIELD	75
——; *West Door and Window*	,, DO.	83
Raglan Castle	,, F. BEDFORD.	88
——; *Grand Staircase*	,, DO.	91
Conway Castle	,, W. R. SEDGFIELD	107
Goodrich Castle	,, F. BEDFORD	125
Fountains Abbey; from the Abbot's House	,, W. R. SEDGFIELD	139
——————; *Lady Chapel*	,, DO.	145
Roslin Chapel; Interior	,, G. W. WILSON	149
——; *'Prentice Pillar*	,, DO.	153
Elgin Cathedral; South Aisle	,, DO.	162
——————; *Choir*	,, DO.	165
Holyrood Abbey; Interior	,, DO.	169
Melrose Abbey; from South West	,, DO.	181
——————; *the Nave*	,, DO.	186
Carisbrooke Castle; the Gateway	,, MCLEAN & MELHUISH	193
——————-; *General View*	,, DO.	201
Rievaux Abbey; Old Gateway	,, W. R. SEDGFIELD	211
Furness Abbey	,, R. FENTON	217
——; *North Transept*	,, DO.	223

Bolton Priory.

FROM Bolton's old monaftic tower,
The bells ring loud with gladfome power;
The fun is bright; the fields are gay
With people in their beft array
Of ftole and doublet, hood and fcarf,
Along the banks of cryftal Wharf;
Through the vale retired and lowly,
Trooping to that fummons holy.
And ah, among the moorlands, fee
What fprinklings of blithe company !
Of laffes and of fhepherd grooms,
That down the fteep hills force their way,
Like cattle through the budded brooms :
Path, or no path, what care they ?
And thus in joyous mood they hie
To Bolton's mouldering Priory.

WORDSWORTH.

OLTON, (fays Dugdale, carefully copied by the " Magna Britannia" of 1731,) a monaftery of regular canons of St. Auguftine, founded in 1120 by Robert de Romeli, Lord of Skipton-in-Craven, and Cecilia his wife, daughter and heir of William de Mefchines, Lord of Coupland in Cumberland, at Emefey, and by them fufficiently endowed. It was dedicated to the Bleffed Virgin and

St. Cuthbert the bishop; and Cecilia, in her widowhood, gave for the souls of her husband, and Ranulph and Matthew, her sons, her whole lordship of Childewick, with the mill and soke thereof, as also of Siglesden and Harwood, with the suit thereof. Alice de Romeli, their daughter, wife of William Fitz-Duncan (1 Henry II., 1151), translated these canons from Emesey to Bolton, which she gave the monks in exchange for other lands of theirs; she being heiress to their founders, confirmed to them all their grants, and further granted free chace in her chace in Craven. King Edward II. (reg. 5,) having all their lands given by their several benefactors recited before him, confirmed them to them. This priory was a cell in some respect to that of Huntington, till it was discharged of that subjection by Pope Celestine III. The prior and convent granted to John de la Insula, or Lisle, Lord of Rougmont, a liberty to found a chantry of six chaplains in the church of Harwood, for the maintenance of which he gave one acre of land, and the advowson of the said church, for the good of his soul, and those of his ancestors. In the reign of king Richard II. (anno. 20), that king granted a licence to Richard de Scrope, knight, to found a chantry of six chaplains, of whom one to be the Custos, in his castle of Bolton, and to endow the same with a yearly rent of £43. 6s. 8d. Other benefactors of this house were William Vavasor, who gave to these monks a carucate and a half of land, with the appurtenances of Fedon; Simon Braam, who gave them a bovate of land in Over-Yeden; and Alice Wentworth, one bovate of land in Wentworth. This priory was surrendered to King Henry VIII.'s visitors, in 1539, by Richard Moon, then prior, when it was found worth £212. 3s. 4d. per annum.

Here the reader has the whole skeleton history of the priory of Bolton, near Skipton-in-Craven, in the style which down to near our own time prevailed amongst topographers; and which often prevails amongſt them now. This was the genuine Dryaſduſt ſyſtem, by which you got the bare bones of the chief facts, and nothing but the bare bones ; no fleſh, no muſcle, no ſkin, no beautifying colour and life. Topographers till the time of ſuch men as Surtees of Durham, Whitaker the hiſtorian of Craven, Baker of Northampton, etc., ſeemed to imagine that nothing was worthy of record but the drieſt facts and genealogies. All thoſe environments of ſcenery which are the life-blood of every place, were left out, and inſtead of a living preſence we were preſented with a corpſe. Who would imagine that in Bolton we had one of the moſt charming ſpots, mingling the lovelieſt art with the lovelieſt nature that England or any other country can ſhow? Whitaker, with a different ſenſe of the unities which conſtitute the actuality of a place, ſays that for picturesque effect the ſite of this Bolton Priory has no equal amongſt northern houſes, and perhaps none in England.

But let us look a little at the ruins of the priory before taking in the whole picture. The ruins, ſurrounded and mingled with magnificent trees, preſent a moſt exquiſite combination of towers, lofty broken arches and gables, with projections and windows of moſt varied character, draped with ivy, and ſtanding on its low green ſward in a noble monaſtic ſolemnity. The different portions of the building diſplay every ſucceſſive ſtyle from the Norman down to the decorated, the final order of Anglo-Gothic. It is evident at a glance that it has been the work of ſucceſſive hands, and ſucceſſive ages. To comprehend the whole the viſitor muſt examine the details for himſelf. We are told that Alice de Romeli,—in 1151, thirty-one years after the period of the foundation,—who had married William Fitz-Duncan, nephew to David king of Scotland, gave this rich and ſheltered ſpot to the monks in exchange for the more bleak and expoſed eſtates of Skipton and Embſey : and that it was on a moſt ſorrowful occaſion, of which we ſhall more particularly ſpeak. The fortunate poſſeſſors did not ceaſe to enlarge improve and enrich their houſe till Henry VIII. broke in upon them, ſtill building, and wreſted the property from Richard Moon, the prior, before he had completed his weſtern tower.

BOLTON PRIORY, WEST END.

The viſitor will be agreeably ſurpriſed to ſee the nave converted into a pariſh church, where divine ſervice is ſtill performed. In different parts of the nave ſtill ſtand five lofty cylindric columns, and equally fine tall lancet windows, with fragments of ſtained glaſs, and beautiful tracery. At the eaſt end of the aiſle of the nave is the old Chantry Chapel, under which is the burial vault of the Claphams and Maulevers of Beamſley. This is covered by eight large rough ſtones, above ſeven feet long, laid ſide by ſide, and riſing nearly two feet above the floor. Theſe old ſquires and knights are ſaid to have been buried upright; and, if we were to believe Wordſworth, you might ſtill ſee them through the chinks of the floor ſtanding grimly in that poſition. But this is at preſent a mere poetical myth, founded, no doubt, on tradition.—

> Paſs, paſs who will yon chantry door,
> And through the chink in the fractured floor
> Look down and ſee a griſly ſight,—
> A vault where the bodies are buried upright!
> There, face by face, and hand by hand,
> The Claphams and Maulevers ſtand;
> And in his place, among ſon and ſire,
> Is John de Clapham, that fierce eſquire,
> A valiant man, and a man of dread
> In the ruthleſs wars of the White and Red;
> Who dragged Earl Pembroke from Banbury church,
> And ſmote off his head on the ſtones of the porch.

The Tudor ſcreen ſeparating the nave from the tranſept remains, and alſo the roof of the nave, painted with broad lines of vermilion, and the beams reſting on figures of angels, one of which ſtands on a creſcent moon,—an evident alluſion to Prior Moon. The choir, in the decorated ſtyle, retains its fine lofty windows, and ſpecimens of tracery of uncommon beauty. On the floor are viſible ſlabs covering the graves of different noble benefactors and priors. Fragments of four of the ſedilia remain, and of a piſcina of the early-Engliſh ſtyle, but greatly mutilated. On the ſouth ſide of the choir are two chapels, which are the reſting-places of the lords of Skipton. In one of them in 1670 was viſible the effigy of the lady Romeli or Romille, the great patroneſs of the houſe. It is ſo no longer. In the old quadrangle ſtands a building appropriated as a ſchool:

and the foundations of the chapter-houfe and of the prior's lodge are yet traceable. The guide-book to the abbey will enable vifitors to notice every particular feature of this fine old pile. In the fields near ftill exifts the priory barn.

"The ruins of this celebrated priory," fays a modern writer, "ftand upon a beautiful curvature of the Wharf, fufficiently elevated to protect it from inundation, and low enough for every purpofe of picturefque effect. Its fite is fo fhut in by hills and embofoming trees, that the ftranger is not aware of it till he is almoft on the fpot." After paffing an ancient, but fnug and comfortable hoftelry,—an agreeable object to thofe who contemplate a fojourn of fome days here,—you crofs a high, bald bridge, very different to the one erected in 1314 by Eve de Laund. On a beam in a cottage adjoining the bridge may be feen this infcription:—

> Thow yat paffys by yes way,
> One ave Maria here now fay.

On your left hand is a large pafture called the Town-field, bounded by the river, in which field, "amid corn almoft ready for the fickle, Prince Rupert, it is faid, on his way to Marfton Moor, encamped in the laft week of July, 1644." The elm under which he dined was remembered in the beginning of the prefent century. Again in 1745, the rebels paftured their horfes there, though it was again laden with corn. There is a pleafant footpath from the bridge, acrofs this fertile plain, to the abbey; but ftrangers generally proceed a few hundred yards further down the road, and enter the abbey-clofe by an opening in the boundary wall, which there remains in good prefervation. There, fome years ago, we entered. We came to a few cottages—to a high ftone wall—to a fmall arched gateway; and paffing through, what a little paradife burft upon us! There were the ruins of the priory amongft magnificent trees; there the river Wharf, fending up a mufical but melancholy found, a flender waterfall thrown from a purple heathery height juft beyond, with the picturefque old parfonage and other houfes lying amongft their trees, and beyond, the wooded valley ftretching away amid rocks and foreft hills, and the old tower of Barden clofing the diftant fcene. What a beau ideal of a rural parfonage was that, with its old ivied porch, and, above it, its ancient efcutcheon on its little tower, its garden and fhrubberies! There then lived the venerable Mr. Carr, the rector, who loved the place like a poet, and had done fo much to open up its beauties to the feet and the eyes of ftrangers. He it was who had conftructed the little chapel in the centre of the trees.—

> In the fhattered fabric's heart
> Remaineth one protected part—
> A rural chapel, neatly dreft,
> In covert like a little neft;
> And thither young and old repair
> On Sabbath-day, for praife and prayer.
> *The White Doe of Rylstone.*

What a day was that. Wordfworth and Whitaker had gone before us, and all the valley and the hills and the air were full of the memories of people and events that made the whole facred ground. There ftood the tower of Richard Moon, the laft prior, who was eclipfed by the burly fhadow of bluff Harry, and left his work unfinifhed. There it ftands, with its fine receding arch embellifhed with fhields and ftatues, and its grand perpendicular window ftands like a fcreen at the weftern entrance. Oppofite is feen the fmall fhooting-lodge of the Duke of Devonfhire, to whom this property has defcended from the Cliffords, and which has been conftructed out of the ancient gateway of the priory.

Crofling the river by large folid ftepping-ftones, we made

our way up that moſt enchanting valley, the charms of which have for years drawn thouſands of viſitors, and ſince the day of railroads hundreds of thouſands. Through woodland ſhades, through wilderneſſes of rock and heather, and ferns and moſſes, and ever and anon coming to a fine view of the dark rapid ſtream below us, or the airy hills around, we made our way to the famous STRID.

The reader is familiar with the ſtory of the young lord of Egremont, who ranging the woods of Bolton, with his greyhounds and huntſmen, and coming to the narrow paſſage where the river pent up rages through in fury, leaped, but having a greyhound in a leaſh, and ſhe a puppy at her heels, the dog hung back, and he was plucked backward, fell in and periſhed. Both Rogers and Wordſworth have celebrated this legend:—

> The pair hath reached that fearful chaſm —
> How tempting to beſtride!
> For lordly Wharf is there pent in
> With rocks on either ſide.
>
> This ſtriding-place is called the STRID—
> A name it took of yore;
> A thouſand years it hath borne that name,
> And ſhall a thouſand more.
>
> And hither is young Romilly come;
> And what may now forbid,
> That he, perhaps for the hundredth time,
> Shall bound acroſs the STRID.
>
> He ſprung in glee, for what cared he
> That the river was ſtrong and the rocks were ſteep?
> But the greyhound in the leaſh hung back,
> And checked him in his leap.
>
> The boy is in the arms of Wharf,
> And ſtrangled by a mercileſs force;
> For never more was young Romilly ſeen,
> Till he roſe a lifeleſs corſe.
>
> *The Force of Prayer.*—WORDSWORTH.

THE STRID.

When the huntſman ſtood before Lady Alice, his mother, he aſked her " What is good for a bootleſs beane ?" (What avails when prayer is uſeleſs ?) And the mother, inſtinctively reading his woe-ſtruck countenance, replied, " Endleſs ſorrow !" And on hearing the fatal truth ſhe became the ſecond foundreſs of Bolton, ſaying, " Many a poor man ſhall be my heir."

> When Lady Aäliza mourned
> Her ſon, and felt in her deſpair
> The pang of unavailing prayer ;
> Her ſon in Wharf's abyſſes drowned,
> The noble boy of Egremond ;
> From which affliction when the grace
> Of God had in her heart found place —
> A pious ſtructure fair to ſee,
> Roſe up, this ſtately priory !

There have been attempts to overthrow this beautiful tradition, by fhowing that when Lady Alice gave her manor of Bolton to the canons, her fon William was, according to a pedigree exhibited in parliament in 1315, fet down as her only fon, and as a party with her to the contract. But we prefer to confider this as relating to the firft foundrefs, giving more faith to a tradition which has clung to the fpot for feven centuries, than to a pedigree exhibited nearly two hundred years after.

Crofling a fine bridge to Barden, we ftood before the old tower of the Cliffords. It is a ruin. "The fhattered remains of Barden Tower," fays Whitaker, "ftand fhrouded in ancient woods, and backed by the purple diftance of the higheft fells. An antiquarian eye refts with pleafure on a view of thatched houfes and barns, which in the laft two centuries have undergone as little change as the fimple and paftoral manners of the inhabitants." So they remained at that moment, yet hence in ages paft iffued,

The ftout Lord Cliffords that did fight in France —

that fought in all the wars of England from the Conqueror to Cromwell. Hence defcended the famous Countefs of Derby, granddaughter of Henry Brandon, Duke of Suffolk, and the fifter of Henry VIII., Queen Dowager of France. Hence Ann Clifford, the renowned Countefs of Pembroke and Montgomery, who lived from the days of Queen Elizabeth to thofe of Charles II., who found fix ruined caftles on her eftates on coming into poffeffion of them, and rebuilt them all, including this tower, of which an infcription in front of it bears teftimony. Her reply to the agent of Charles II., who prefumed to dictate a candidate for the borough of Appleby, deferves to live for ever:—

"I have been bullied by a ufurper; I have been neglected by

a court; but I will not be dictated to by a subject. Your man shan't stand.

"ANNE, DORSETT, PEMBROKE, AND MONTGOMERY."

But no anceſtral ſpot bears a more ſingular record than that of the Shepherd Lord. This was the ſon of Lord John Clifford, called the bloody or black-faced Clifford, who fell at the battle of Towton. His mother was obliged to fly and hide him, a mere child, from the vengeance of Edward IV., and bring him up as a ſhepherd in the wildeſt receſſes of Yorkſhire and Cumberland. Growing up in this condition to man's eſtate, when the attainder was reverſed by Henry VII., he came and ſettled here, to be near the monks of Bolton, by whom his neglected education was repaired. With them he contracted a great friendſhip, and ſtudied with them aſtronomy, and, no doubt, aſtrology as well as alchemy. The people believed ſtrange things of him.

> He knew the rocks which angels haunt
> On the mountains viſitant.
> He hath kenned them taking wing :
> And the caves where fairies ſing
> He hath entered ; and been told
> By voices how men lived of old.
> Among the heavens his eye can ſee
> Face of thing that is to be ;
> And if men report him right,
> He could whiſper words of might.
>
> WORDSWORTH.

Writings preſerved in the archives of the Cliffords, writings attributed to him, ſay as much, and hint at myſteries that cannot be ſpoken, ſuch as the ſecret of gold-making.

> Hie wer accurſyde that ſoo wolde done
> How ſchold yow have ſervans then,
> To tyll your lands, and dryffe your plughe ?
> Yff ev'ry mane to ryches came,
> Then none for oth'r owght wolde dowghe.

But it is over Rylſton Fells that falls the deepeſt enchantment of poetry. It was over theſe heathery fells that the White Doe uſed to take her way. On them ſtands the remains of the old tower of the Nortons, where the ſtout Richard Norton gave to the winds his ſtandard, ſurrounded by his nine ſons, in " The Riſing in the North." Thence he bore the banner wrought by his only daughter, on which were diſplayed the croſs,

<blockquote>And the five wounds our Lord did bear.</blockquote>

In this poem Wordſworth has put forth a chivalrous ſtrength and drawn a picture of devotedneſs in the father and in his ſon Francis, which, though oppoſed in its object, is equally noble.

Such are the memories which have caſt their golden glory over Bolton Priory; the Vale of Wharf; over the Strid; over Barden Tower and Norton Tower on the grim Rylſton Fells, and inveſted them with an intereſt to all time.

Glastonbury Abbey.

GLASTONBURY ABBEY, now reduced to a few ruined walls, had the diftinguifhed honour of being the firft church founded in Britain. "Eft enim," fays John of Glaftonbury, "omnium in Anglia ecclefiarum prima et vetuftiffima, primo ex virgis torquatis facta, ex qua virtus divinæ fanctitatis jam inde à principio redolevit fpiravitque in omnem patriam." It is the firft and moft ancient of all churches in England, originally conftructed out of twifted withes, but from which the virtue of divine fanctity has already from this beginning breathed its fragrance over the whole country. This monkifh hiftorian of the then proud abbey, in the fifteenth century, tells us that it was called by the Englifh EALDECHIRCHE, that is the ancient church, and that the people of that province found nothing by which they might fwear an oath fo facred that they fhould fear to break it, as the ancient church; and that it was equally eminent by the reverence of its antiquity and of its magnificently exalted fanctity. "It was called a fecond Rome."

John of Glaftonbury—whofe chronicle was edited by Hearne, the antiquarian, from the MS. in the Afhmolean Library—tells us that he availed himfelf of the labours of William of Malmsbury, who wrote the chronicle of the abbey from its foundation by Jofeph of Arimathea, in the fixty-third year of our Lord's incarnation, the thirty-firſt after his paſſion, to the time of the Abbot Henry Bleys, biſhop of Wincheſter, in the year 1126; of the brother Adam of Domerham, a monk of this houſe, down to the time of John of Tantonia, the lord abbot, in the year 1290; interſperſing certain matters from Giraldus Cambrenſis and Radulph of Cheſter; that he abbreviated the prolixity of the ſaid Adam, omitting, adding, and reducing facts to their proper order; that he had endeavoured to follow the truth, though in a rude ſtyle and with uncultivated language—" Rudi quidem ſtilo, et ſermone inculto,"—rightly thinking that " melior is veritas in ſimplicibus verbis, quam ſit mendacium in venuſtate ſermonis."

And truly, if the veracity of our hiſtorian is equal to the rudeneſs of his Latin, more reliable narrative was never written. He gives us ulcio for ultio, eciam for etiam, *way*viatores for viatores; in fact, in almoſt every place ſubſtituting c for t, with phraſes oft recurring of tolerable Engliſh with Latin terminations; with michi for mihi, nichil for nihil. And with what a ſimple faith our good chronicler relates his carefully-ſifted facts. This is his account of the circumſtances which led Joſeph of Arimathea to Glaſtonbury:—The Lord being crucified, and all things accompliſhed which were foretold by the prophets, Joſeph of Arimathea, that noble decurion (a commander of ten men, about equivalent to a corporal,) went to Pilate and begged the body of Jeſus, and wrapped it in fine linen, and laid it in a monument in which no man had yet been buried. Now the Jews hearing of this, ſought " apprehendere eum ;" and with him Nicodemus and others. Theſe all hid themſelves except Joſeph and Nicodemus, who appeared, and demanded why they were angry becauſe they had buried the Lord, and whether they had not yet reflected how much good he had done, and how ill

Access key: L/A5\3007037
Records not in database
Access key: T/RUINED ABBEYS AND CASTLES OF GREAT BRITAIN
11 records retrieved
Enter Alt List commands
:12
    CA:uocR RSN=41112240
    OB:uocR RSN=41.3525
End of list reached
Enter nit list commands
RSN/ABS: not active
RSN/ASN: 41-112-240
transfer from passive?
Y

they had done in crucifying him? Whereupon they seized Joseph and Nicodemus and shut them up in a chamber without a window, and gave the key to Annas and Caiaphas, and placed guards at the door. Nicodemus they soon set at liberty; but they determined to put Joseph to death because he had begged the body of Jesus, and had been the chief instigator of his burial. Being assembled to determine what death he should die, they commanded Annas and Caiaphas to produce him; but on opening the chamber they found that he was not there. In great consternation they sent messengers everywhere to learn news of him, and he was found quietly residing in his native city of Arimathea.

At this wonderful discovery the chief priests consulted how they were to induce him to come back; and "tollentes thomum cartæ,"—which, in Glastonbury Latin, means taking a sheet of paper,—they wrote to him confessing their great sins against him, and imploring him to come to his fathers and to his sons, who were all filled with admiration of his divine assumption; adding " Peace be with thee, Joseph, honoured of all the people." And they chose seven men, friends of Joseph, to carry this epistle, and honourably to salute the holy man on delivering it. Joseph kissed the messengers, took them into his house, and thanked God who had thus changed his enemies and the crucifiers of Christ. "Alia autem die ascendit super asinum suum, et ambulavit cum illis, et venit Jerusalem." That is, the next day he got upon his ass, and ambled with them, and came to Jerusalem. The Jews assembling all kissed Joseph, and Nicodemus received him into his house, and made him a feast, and Annas and Caiaphas in full Sanhedrim inquired respectfully by what means he had been conveyed away from the chamber that was so well locked and guarded. Whereupon Joseph informed them that, as he was at his devotions in the prison, at midnight, the house was suspended in the air by four angels, and the Lord Jesus appeared to him in a glory of light, and lifting him from the earth to which he had fallen, took him by the hand, washed him with rose-water, wiped his face, kissed him, and said to him (dixit michi), "Be not afraid Joseph, I am Jesus." He then showed Joseph the place where he had buried him, and the linen in which he had wrapped him, and the napkin in which he had folded his head, as a proof that he was the Lord; and then conducted him home to his house in Arimathea, bidding him not to go out for forty days, and so disappeared.

This account seems to have charmed the Jews; and as for Joseph, he betook himself to the evangelist Philip, and was baptised with his son Joseph. Afterwards he was delegated by St. John, whilst he was labouring among the Ephesians, to become the Para-nymph or devotee of the blessed and perpetual Virgin Mary, and of her glorious virgin assumption. And he joined St. Philip and other disciples who had seen and known the Lord Jesus and his mother Mary, and they preached through various regions, converting and baptizing many people, till, in the fifteenth year after the assumption of the blessed Virgin, he came with his son Joseph, whom the Lord Jesus had consecrated as bishop in the city of Shiraz, to the apostle Philip in Gaul. Philip, desirous to preach the gospel, sent twelve of his disciples, including his beloved friend Joseph and his son Joseph, into Britain, Joseph being put at their head. Five hundred men and women set forth with Joseph under vows of chastity, which however they broke, and only a hundred and fifty were allowed to accompany the saint. These by the command of the Lord set sail on the night of the Lord's ascension, on Joseph's shirt, which he spread for them, and arrived in Britain the next morning. But the sinners having repented, at the prayers of Jofeph, the Lord fent a fhip which had been fcientifically built by Solomon, fo that it might laft till the time of Chrift. With them came Mordraius, a king of the Medes, and his general Vacianus, both of whom Jofeph had formerly baptized in the city of Shiraz ; for the Lord appeared to Mordraius in a vifion, and fhewed him that the perfidious king of North Wales had caft Jofeph into a dungeon for preaching Chriftianity. Mordraius and his general Vacianus marched againft him with an army, flew him, and liberated Jofeph : upon which they all returned great thanks amongft much joy to God.

After this Jofeph and his fon travelled throughout Britain, where reigned king Arviragus, a barbarian, who with his people forbad them to preach the Chriftian faith. Yet, after a time, beholding the modefty of their lives, he gave to Jofeph and his eleven religious brethren, including his fon Jofeph, equalling the number of the apoftles, a certain ifland called YNSWITRYN, —that is, Infula Vitrea,—fituated amid woods, thickets and marfhes, and thus called on account of a ftream which flowed round it through the marfhes which was of the colour of glafs, —whence the name of the place became Glaftonbury, or the city of glafs. It was alfo called the Ifle of Avalon, from Aval the Britifh name for an apple, being very prolific of that fruit. And this name of Avalon became very famous, not only on account of the monaftery, but alfo that it was the burial-place of king Arthur. The fettling of Jofeph here was celebrated by a monkifh poet in the following lines :—

> Intrat Avalloniam duodena caterva virorum.
> Flos Armathiæ Jofeph eft primes eorum.
> Jofephes, ex Jofeph genitus, patrem comitatur.
> His aliifque decem jus Glaftoniæ propriatur.

Here Jofeph was directed by the archangel Gabriel in a vifion to build a church in honour of the mother of God, the perpetual Virgin Mary; and he pointed out to him the spot. In obedience to the archangel he conftructed it in a circular form of plaited twigs, no doubt of willow, which muft have been abundant there,—a fort of bafket-work church. This was in the thirty-firft year after the paffion of our Saviour.

Here the holy brethren continued for years to ferve God and the holy Virgin in watchings, fafts, and facred exercifes, fo that Marius the fon of Arviragus, and Coilus the fon of Marius, granted them twelve hides of land around their humble oratory—a hide each. In courfe of time Jofeph and his companions died. The fpot was not chofen with much reference to fanitary principles; it muft have been very damp and unwholefome: their lives probably were not long. Jofeph was buried in a bifurcate line from the meridian angle of the oratory, in prepared hurdles, lying upon a figure of the adorable Virgin, " and having interred with him two veffels of filver filled with the blood and fweat of the prophet Jefus, by virtue of which neither water nor the dew of heaven can ever be wanting to the inhabitants of this moft noble ifle. When his farcophagus fhall be opened, which will be in the valley of Jofaphat fometime before the day of judgment, it will be found to have been untouched, and be fhown to the whole world."

After the death of Jofeph and his eleven companions the place continued long deferted, and from the abode of holy men became once more a lair of wild beafts, till it pleafed the holy Virgin to recall her oratory to the memory of the faithful. Yet the race of Jofeph of Arimathea was not extinct; on the contrary, it became the royal line, and the famous king Arthur was the tenth in defcent from him. According to the book called the *Sanctum Graal*, this was the genealogy:— Helaius, the nephew of Jofeph, was the father of Jofhua, Jofhua of Aminadab, and fo in fucceffion followed Caftellors, Manuel, Lambord, and a fon not named, who was the father of Ygernam, who was the father of Uther Pendragon, the father of the renowned king Arthur.

A hundred years had paffed over, and paganifm ftill covered the kingdom of Britain, when king Lucius fent to Eleutherius, the thirteenth pope from St. Peter, defiring him to fend Chriftian preachers. Eleutherius accordingly fent two holy men, Phaganus and Diruvianus, who arrived juft one hundred and three years after the coming of Jofeph and his companions. Led by God, they entered the wildernefs of Avalon, and difcovered the remains of a crofs and other figns identifying the place which God had chofen to be the firft church of his Son Jefus and of the mother of Jefus in thefe realms. With much joy they rebuilt the oratory, and twelve brethren continued to live there; their places at their death being filled up by fucceffors, till St. Patrick, the apoftle of Ireland, became the firft abbot of Glaftonbury : and thirty years' indulgence was granted by pope Eleutherius to all Chriftians from other parts of Britain who vifited Glaftonbury ; thus confirming the faith amongft the Britons. Phaganus and Diruvianus had built a new oratory of ftone, which they dedicated to Chrift and the apoftles Peter and Paul ; and, by direction of the Lord, they alfo erected an oratory to St. Michael on the top of the hill in the ifland, to the laft of which thofe feeking the grand indulgence had to make their pilgrimage.

Such is the ftory of the founding of the mother church of England according to John of Glaftonbury. Such were the legends by which the earlier Roman Catholics fatisfied the fimple faith of the people great and fmall. We are afraid that the narrative will not agree very well with the hiftory of the early Britifh church, which admitted no claims of Rome at this period, and denied both its affumptions and many of its doctrines. Quite as little is it to be expected that the Irifh proteftants will concede that the great faint of that ifland, St. Patrick, after his converfion of the Hibernians, came over to Glaftonbury, and lived and died its firft abbot, in full communion with the papal church. Such a verfion we muft refer to the monk Jofcelin of Furnefs Abbey, who wrote the life of St. Patrick in the twelfth century, and firft converted him into a Roman faint. That and the next age was a time when the Roman hierarchy in Britain, as in other places, was bufy deftroying the churches and fchools of the primitive church; and then, after fome of them had been five hundred years in their graves, made faints of the very men who had ftood the boldeft adverfaries of all Italian corruptions or affumptions; namely, Patrick, or as originally called Succat; Columbkille, Kevin, Columbanus, Gallus, Claude Clement, Erigena, Albinus, Virgilius, and a hoft of others. The truth feems to have been, that at an early day primitive Chriftianity was driven out of England into Ireland, and thence to Iona, and returned thence again to both England and the continent through the apoftles of the Irifh fchool of Bangor, and of the venerable Iona. As for Ireland, St. Bernard of Clairvaux, in his life of Malachy, bifhop of Down, fays that he and the monks fent over thither by Bernard himfelf, were " the firft true monks Ireland ever faw." And this is fully confirmed by archbifhop Ufher, who fays that Malachy, archbifhop of Armagh, and Laurence of Dublin, both in the twelfth century, were the firft bifhops of Ireland canonized by the pope.

Yet it is amufing with what gravity John of Glaftonbury tells us that he was fent by Pope Cæleftinus in 425 to convert the Irifh—that having refufed to be made pope himfelf, he landed in Cornwall, and went thence to Glaftonbury in 433, having in the meantime converted the Irish nation with many portents and miracles—that is, in eight years. There he found the twelve brethren, who hailed him abbot. St. Patrick in a charter which he granted, containing an indulgence of one hundred days to all pilgrims thither, is made to tell us that he found in the monastery, the Acts of the Apostles and the Acts of Phaganus and Diruvianus. Patrick, says John of Glastonbury, lived to the age of one hundred and eleven, having been abbot thirty-nine years.

There has run a legend that Joseph of Arimathea on arriving at Glastonbury struck down his walking-stick, an Asiatic thorn, whilst he prayed, and behold, it shot out boughs, leaves, and flowers, and continued to flourish there as the famous Glastonbury thorn till the destruction of the monastery by Henry VIII. But it seems that this miracle attended St. Benignus, the adopted son and immediate successor of St. Patrick. Benignus having been for seven years educated in Rome, despising the prospect of pontifical dignity which it appears—he, like St. Patrick also had, and warned by an angel, set out on a pilgrimage. He was led by God to Glastonbury, where he found his patron St. Patrick, and to whom he told his divine mission. St. Patrick said, " Go on, my beloved son, contented with thy staff. And when thou comest to the spot where the Lord has predestined thee to settle, strike thy staff into the earth, and it shall shoot forth, grow verdurous, and blossom." Benignus, therefore, made a long travel through forests, moors, and marshes, but the stick did not shoot into life till he came again to Glastonbury, where, our historian tells us, it continued to his own day growing a large and spreading tree close to the oratory of the saint.

From the time of St. Patrick and of this miracle the fame of Glastonbury grew rapidly. Many kings, queens, princes, and generals defired to be buried there, becaufe the founder, St. Jofeph, had buried the Lord. Continually new grants of eftates and privileges were made to it by kings and great men and women, till in time it became the moft wealthy and magnificent monaftery, as well as the moft ancient, in the kingdom. Amongft the principal donors of land were king Arthur, king Domp, king Cenewalch, king Baldred, Wilfrid archbifhop of York, king Kinewulph, king Ina, who built the great church, king Offa, king Egbert, king Athelwulf, king Alfred, queen Elfleda, king Edwin, king Edgar, king Edmund Ironfides, Edward the Elder, and Edward the Younger, king Canute, befides many other kings, queens, dukes, and noble men and ladies.

Amongft the chief perfons interred in the church and the cemetery were numbers of faints and bifhops, as well as kings; of courfe, Jofeph of Arimathea and his fon, the bifhop of Shiraz, Phaganus and Diruvianus, the reftorers of the place; St. Dunftan, one of the moft famous of Glaftonbury abbots, and archbifhop of Canterbury, renowned for his pinching the devil's nofe with hot tongs, but by his cotemporaries more renowned for his active genius. He built a fmall room near the oratory, where he worked. He wrote, he painted, he carved cups and croffes and other articles, as well as made veftments for the mafs, which our author fays were kept to his time. He was deeply verfed in hiftorical ballads, and the magical fongs of the Saxons, regarded in thofe dark times with peculiar horror. St. Urban the pope and martyr lay there, faints Appollinarius a difciple of the apoftle Peter, and Ofwald, Patrick, Benignus, Aidan, bifhop of Lindisfarne, the Venerable Bede; the bones of St. Gildas the hiftorian, of St. Hilda, abbefs of Whitby, and of many other abbeffes and fainteffes.

As for kings and great men, fuch were the numbers brought

hither to be buried, that the whole pavement of the church, even about the high altar, above it and below it, and on each fide, and thofe of the two chapels, and the furface of the whole cemetery, were fo crowded by them that it was difficult to find place for any other. And thofe who lived in diftant regions, even to a certain Soldan, fent for its facred earth to be buried with them. Here king Arthur, who was fond of feeking reft and retirement from the cares of government at the abbey, died of a wound received from his nephew, the ufurper Modred, in Cornwall, and was buried in the cemetery about the year of our Lord 542. Nine feet deep was he buried, left the Saxons his enemies, whom he had fo often conquered, fhould find and infult his remains. On a leaden crofs, however, placed under the ftone which covered him, and with the writing turned next to the ftone for concealment, was infcribed:—" Hic jacet fepultus inclitus rex Arthurus in infula Avallonia, cum Guennevera uxore fua fecunda." But Guennever was buried fometime after, and placed over king Arthur, only fix feet deep. Six hundred years afterwards his remains, at the repeated inftigation of Henry II., were fought for and found, as well as thofe of his queen Guennever. The crofs and infcription were entire. The bones of the king were of an enormous fize ; and the hair of the queen ftill looking frefh and enveloping her bones, yet falling to powder on being touched. Thefe were transferred to the church and buried in feparate tombs ; that of the queen being at the foot of that of the king, before the high altar. Here Edward the Firft, and Elinor the queen, coming in 1278, had thefe tombs opened, and found all as before defcribed. The king then wrapped the bones of Arthur in a rich pall, and the queen did the fame by thofe of Guennever, and replaced them in their tombs, fealing them with their feals. But they retained the fcull and the legs of each, to place on the tombs for the devotion of the people, with an infcription commemorating thefe facts. Both our great Edwards vifited Glaftonbury. Edward III., with his queen Philippa, in 1331, came with a princely train, and on leaving prefented the abbey £80, and four filver cups, one very magnificent, and an embofled water jug alfo of filver.

As for facred relics collected at Glaftonbury, their mere catalogue would make a little book. They included almoft everything in facred hiftory.—Fragments from the tomb of Rachel; the altar of Mofes; the rod of Mofes; the manna of the children of Ifrael; the fepulchres of Ifaiah and Daniel; the remains of the three men in the fiery furnace, of the fwaddling-clothes of our Saviour; two portions of the very manger in which he lay; the ftone from Jordan on which Chrift ftood to be baptized; one of the ftones offered by the devil when he defired Chrift to command the ftones to be made bread; one of the water-jars in which our Lord turned the water into wine; a piece of the bread with which he fed the five thoufand; a piece of the ftone on which he ftood in the temple, of his garment without a feam, of the robe that Herod put upon him, of the fcourge with which he was fcourged, of the table at which he fupped with his difciples, of the fponge offered to him with vinegar, of the crofs, the fepulchre, of the hole in which the crofs ftood; one of the thorns from his crown; the ftone from which he afcended into heaven, and of every other imaginable thing connected with his hiftory. And the fame of the Virgin Mary, of the apoftles, of John the Baptift and all the martyrs, the faints by hundreds, and holy virgins by dozens. The lift of thefe relics by John of Glaftonbury fills feventeen clofely-printed octavo pages.

What a pile of mendacious rubbifh with which to gull the fimple fouls of thofe dark times! Thefe were the baits with which the Romiſh Church then fought to draw people to what they called Chriſtianity. Can any one wonder that, as foon as light dawned, all thefe fpurious trumperies, all the lying miracles which kept them company, and of which we have moſt ludicrous examples in our chronicler John, and all the purgatorial inventions following after them, ſhould not only move difguſt, but tend to deſtroy faith in the real miracles, and the real hereafter of revelation? The blow given to a vital faith in Chriſtianity by the Church of Rome by thefe bafe and felfiſh arts, and of which their own hiſtorians are the atteſtors, is felt even in the prefent day, in the feeble credence of profeſſed believers, and in the vaſt fpread of a hopelefs materialifm.

Sailors at fea bait for fiſh with a mere bit of red rag, the mockery of a piece of fleſh; but the Romaniſts of the middle ages baited for fouls with more empty and faplefs things. Yet for the cupidity of the rich and powerful, God made them unconfciouſly and blindly bait with fubſtantial temptations. Their vaſt hoarded wealth, their gold and filver veſſels, their ſhrines garniſhed and loaded with jewels, their pictures by the greateſt maſters, and ſtill more their magnificent eſtates, drew the eyes and hearts of kings and nobles even as they pretended to worſhip, and at length they laid rapacious hands on the whole ſtupendous prey. The fyſtem was built on the delufive fands of impofition, and when the floods and tempeſts of fecular power beat upon it, it fell, and great was the fall thereof. What a moral in this worldlinefs! The very things which they imagined were building up their ſtrength were preparing their deſtruction.

What a right royal eſtate did that of Glaſtonbury grow to! From the wicker church and the ten hides of marſhy, thicketty land—in the time of the abbot Richard Beere, in the year

1507, and the eighteenth of the reign of Henry VII., the abbey had grown into a moft magnificent pile, full of opulence and dead men's bones, and its lands and lordfhips to an amplitude which required a volume merely to enumerate them. Such a volume the abbot Richard Beere had compiled from

GLASTONBURY ABBEY, CHANTRY CHAPEL.

actual furveys and perambulations, which was duly preferved in the abbey library, of which the mere extracts given by John of Salifbury amount to fixty-fix pages. Thomas Sutton, "humilimus, quanquam lonnge indignus, hujus facri cœnobii profeſſus, officium gerens cellerarii forinfici," who wrote the book called the "Terrarium cœnobii Glaftonienfis," tells us with what labour the work was done:—how the noble abbot called in the affiftance of men not only "induftrios et diligentes, verum eciam magnos, eruditos et fapientes;" namely, John Fitzjames, armiger and learned in the law, and fenefchal of Glaftonbury; William Lange, auditor and præpofitor; with John Horner, the land-furveyor, a prudent man, and bailiff of Whitftone, with other affifting menfurants; Thomas Somerfet and William Walton clerks of the treafury.

The enumeration and defcription of the eftates belonging to the abbey were enough to make the mouth of a much lefs rapacious monarch than Harry VIII. water. Such fine old manors, —Glaftonbury, Eftrete, Weft Pennard, Godenye, Mere, Northlode, Eftbrent, Therlefmere, Lymplefhame, Southbrent, Berghes, Wryngton, Hunftert, Merkyfbury, &c. At thefe manors were noble manor-houfes, churches, chapels, vineyards, mills, lakes and pools for fifh, immenfe moors for firewood and game, parks, ftreams, quarries of ftone, orchards for fruit, and every imaginable thing that can make a very princedom. The monarchs of thofe times might well have afked with James of Scotland, "What want thefe knaves that a king fhould have?" Within the manor of Glaftonbury proper we are told that there was not only the princely abbey, but all requifite buildings for the adminiftration of juftice, for holding feffions and trying criminals; for the abbey had all the rights of a lordly jurifdiction held by charter of Edmund, namely, "libertatem et poteftatem, jura et confuetidines, et omnes forisfacturas omnium terrarum fuarum; id eft, Burgbrice, Hundredfocna, Athas, Ordelas, Infangenetheofas, Frithbrice, Foreftealle, et Toll et Team; et fint terræ fuæ fibi liberæ, et folutæ ab omni calumpnia, ficut meæ michi habentur." Which barbarous terms would require a little volume of legal expofition to fet forth all their fulnefs of power and privileges. But, in fhort, they held all thefe lands free of the king or of any feudal lord whatever; had all the rights of thief-taking and hanging when taken, of holding and letting lands by common foccage, of exercifing all rights of water as well as of land; rights of fifh and foreft, of levying toll at their mills, and of compelling every one in their vicinity to grind at their mills. On the manor of Glaftonbury alone there were four mills—a water mill, a wind-mill, a horfe-mill, and a fulling-mill. Still more, they had the right of compelling the tenants to do their team-work, to draw their fuel and other neceffaries, and to do their ploughing and fowing and harvefting at a certain price. Moreover certain tenants were bound to do what was called lundmary, or Monday-work, and were called Mondaymen. They were bound every year, fummer and winter, to work forty days for the lord abbot for fix hours a-day, at whatever work and where he chofe, and not when they chofe, at an obolus or halfpenny a-day, amounting each man to twenty-pence the year. "Opera cuftumariorum tenentium Domini ibidem, vocata Moundayewarkes, facta et facienda per diverfos tenentes, vocatos Mondaymen; videlicet quod quilibet eorum, ex antiqua confuetudine, annuatim per quadraginta dies, per miniftros Domini eis affignatos et limitatos, ad placitum Domini, et non ad libitum tenentium, operabitur quadraginta dies yemales et æftivales, qualibet die inde operando et bene laborando per fex horas integras cujuslibet diei eis affignati, capiendo quilibet eorum, quando fic operatur, obolum, cujus fumma eft xx*d*. per annum."

Some alfo worked eight days during the autumn, having, no doubt during the harveft, a penny a-day. The cuftoms varied in other manors; in fome, all tenants without exception working at the call of the lord abbot, for more or lefs days, and in default paying a fixed fine. Befides thefe, there were by ancient cuftom other men who worked on the moors, called Moormen or Chalengelondmen, who cut down, carried, ftacked, and cut up for ufe, wood for the lord's fires, working at this eleven days each year, at a penny a-day. Thefe moormen, or Chalengelondmen, had to clear the water-courfes and mend and make walls for fences; others dreffed the vineyards, for they had fuch then, and grew the vegetables on the fame terms, and drew the wine and other provifions to the abbey by wagon or in boats.

To the abbey belonged vaft parks for deer and other animals. The parks of Wyralle and Sherpehame are particularly mentioned, as well as the vineyard of Wyralle. This park, it fays, contains three hundred and twenty-two acres; "in which park" the lord abbot Richard had newly erected an exceedingly beautiful manor-houfe, with chapel, eating-rooms, chambers, butteries, kitchen, and adorned with all other neceffary apartments; the front of the manor being enclofed by ftone walls, and the reft by fawn oak pales. To which adjoined an orchard, ftews for fifh, etc. In this park, three hundred deer, and forty larger animals might be maintained, and hawking could annually be purfued in the furrounding meadows of one hundred and fifty-two acres.

There was alfo in this manor a moor called Hultemoor, of two hundred and feventy-three acres; another moor, Hethmoor, or the heathery moor, of eight hundred acres; a third moor, Southmoor or Allermoor, that is Aldermoor, of one thoufand one hundred and forty acres, which was formerly incapable of being hunted, from the thicknefs of the aldertrees, but was then grazed by the tenants, and furnifhed fuel for the monaftery; and a fourth moor, of four hundred and thirty acres, called Kynnyard Moor. In this one manor, therefore, there were park and moorlands for chafe, grazing, and fuel, to the amount of nearly three thoufand acres. In what a lordly and yet Nimrod folitude muft thefe jolly monks have lived !

The lakes and pools for fifh and wild-fowl were numerous, and fome of them of vaft extent. That of Mere alone was a mile long and three-quarters of a mile broad. There were "gurgites," not as you would fuppofe whirlpools, but weirs where fifheries for eels and other fifh were carried on. Some of thefe, as Lichelake or Cockfmere, were let for as much as one hundred and fix fhillings and eightpence per annum,—a great fum then. There were alfo large woods on the different manors, and copfes; and on all thefe manors were pleafant manor-houfes, with all appurtenances. That of Eftbrent may ferve as an image of them all. It had chapel, hall, dining-room, chambers high and low, buttery, cellar, bakehoufe, kitchen, larder, a dome on the fouth fide of the kitchen called the wodehoufe, with chambers above, called giften chambers, and various other chambers nobly built, with a fumptuous portico, bearing the abbatial arms, with a garden of an acre enclofed by hewn oak paling of eight feet high. In the exterior court, "unum ftabulum, cum folario (fundial) et hayhoufe, cum penfald." On the north fide was an orchard of the choiceft apples and pears, and other fine fruits, of three acres one perch, furrounded by elms and oaks of a wonderful height and bulk, where the herons built and reared their young. At Wryngton manor the orchard was eleven acres eleven perches, with barns and granges, and cattle-ftalls, and dovecotes; and a lodge before the great gate, called Goggeboure, rented by William Trewbody. Befides all thefe, there were numerous farms and villages bringing in ample rents, and quarries of freeftone—"Quarrura pretrarum liberarum, vocat freeftone"—with other mills and fulling-houfes, with fines and dues of various kinds.

What a growth from the wicker church and the ten hides

of land! That magnificent abbey with its many gables and peaked roofs, grey with age; its lofty church carved and crocketed, and folemn with heaven-feeking pinnacles, and faint-and-king-peopled niches : with its lofty aifles and foaring columns, its gnofped and rofe-centred arches; its pavements floried with the mementos of the great dead; its organed choir; its gold-fretted altar; its gorgeous-hued windows; its chanters and incenfe; and all around its lands, and hamlets, and forefts.

On all this glory came down the rude hand of Henry VIII. What a fhock and aftonifhment was that which went through the realm! Thefe proud houfes, proud in affumed humility; thefe lordly mitred abbots and priors, thefe felf-folacing monks and friars, this fyftem which feemed bafed on the eternities— fuddenly fhaken, fhattered, hurled down. Thofe fertile lands, thofe chace-haunted moors, thofe folemn woods, thofe pleafant and lordly nefts of devotion lapped in luxury,—all grafped and appropriated by hungry and hard-handed barons and fupple courtiers : and a new and mightier ariftocracy built on the ruins of the church. Not a fragment of them left for the poor: not that third which the church profeffed to dedicate to the poor: but clergy and laity, almoners and alms-recipients at the buttery door, all turned adrift together. It was as if the very pillars of the earth had given way; and a wide howling and roaring mifery was left behind. That ˊmifery and the crimes engendered by it outlived the great defpoiler, Harry. In vain he hanged the homelefs vagabonds by thoufands yearly. They outlived him and his fon, and his eldeft daughter, and compelled, at length, the lion-hearted queen Befs to reftore the portion of the poor by the Poor-law Act of the thirty-fourth year of her reign.

And now, after the flight of three hundred and more years,

that great revolution is but as a tale that is told. The moſſed and ivied walls of abbey and monaſtery remain alone to ſay that ſuch things were; once ſacred, now only picturesque: and we who now enjoy thoſe once ſacred lands, imagine, like their quondam conventual poſſeſſors, that our ſtatus is ſecure as the earth beneath us, and that we ſhall never be moved: dreaming not of the ſocial revolutions in the boſom of time—of the perpetual elements of change in the heart of ſociety; and that, from period to period, " Sic tranſit gloria mundi."

Amongſt the more remarkable hiſtorical events and cuſtoms of the place we may note the following. The Abbot Herlewinus is ſuppoſed to have built the exquiſite chapel of St. Joſeph. He had been a monk at Caen in Normandy, where he had been converſant with the fineſt Norman architecture of his time. He built a noble church, and was of ſo hoſpitable a diſpoſition, that he threatened to deprive the porter of the abbey of his ears, if he drove from its gates pilgrims without relief. William of Malmeſbury ſays that ſo early as ſeven hundred and nineteen ſuch was the magnificence of this abbey, that it had a chapel plated over with two thouſand ſix hundred and forty lbs. of ſilver; and had an altar of gold of the weight of two hundred and forty-ſix lbs., with many precious gems and coſtly robes.

Such was the power aſſumed by the abbots, and their ſtrict aſſertion of their rights, that when King Edward I. paid his viſit, the abbot would not admit him till he had appointed his own ſheriff of the twelve hides, and his own earl-marſhal, leſt, by the king exerciſing any ſovereign rights, the chartered privileges of the abbey ſhould be impaired. Neither would he allow him to hold an aſſize at Glaſtonbury, but the king was obliged to hold it in the village of Street, beyond the boundaries of the abbot's juriſdiction.

Theſe noble buildings received much damage at different

times. In 1184, much of them was deftroyed by fire, but they were rebuilt under the munificent patronage of Henry II. During the abbacy of Adam de Sodbury, an earthquake, in 1276, threw down many of the monaftic buildings, and great part of St. Michael's church on the fummit of Tor-hill. The abbey itfelf this fpirited abbot rebuilt, adding alfo the beautiful chapel of St. Mary, which terminated the eaft end of the church, adorning it with gorgeoufly painted windows, and many valuable gifts of gold, filver, and precious ftone. The church when complete was five hundred and ninety-four feet in length, or two hundred and twenty-three feet longer than the cathedral of Wells. The abbey poffeffed a valuable library. We have a catalogue of it as it exifted in the time of John of Glaftonbury; and Leland, who faw it about fixteen years before its deftruction, fays:—" No fooner had I croffed the threfhold of this library, than the fight alone of fo many ancient works ftruck my mind with devout aftonifhment, fo that I even drew back amazed. Then, after faluting the prefiding deity, for many days I remained examining its burdened fhelves." There were fplendid copies of the fcriptures of the Fathers, the Cafuifts, the hiftories of Bede and Gildas, moft of the Greek and Roman claffics, Gefta of the Normans, of the popes, of the Fall of Troy, Lives and Miracles of the Saints, Paffionals of the Saints, Libri Prognofticorum, the Enigmata of St. Aldhelm, and the Didafcaligon of Hugo. Befides thefe, there was an extenfive collection of charters conferred on the abbey, and miffals, breviaries, paffionals, antiphonalia, etc., moft fuperbly written and illuminated by the monks. They had a fine large room, called the Scriptorium, in which they carried on their literary and artiftic labours. The Rev. J. Williams, in his account of Glaftonbury Abbey, fays, " In goldfmiths' work and jewellery inftances of their moft beauteous workmanship still remain. Their caligraphy is unrivalled, as exemplified in ancient documents and charters. The illuminations of their missals are not now to be matched; nor can modern artists surpass their painted glass in the intensity and permanence of its gorgeous colouring. An astronomical clock, made by Lightfoot, monk of Glastonbury, is still preserved in Wells cathedral."

The monks of Glastonbury were Benedictines, and their rules were very severe; but there is abundant historical evidence that for a long time they had not been too austere in the observance of these rules; which otherwise demanded that they should perform their devotions seven times in the twenty-four hours. During Lent they fasted every day until six in the evening, and were then compelled to shorten the usual time of sleeping. They slept in the dormitory in separate rooms, and always in their clothes. During the day they were obliged to go two and two together. They never conversed at their meals, but listened to the reading of the Scriptures. For small faults they were expelled for a short time from the refectory; for greater ones they were debarred from public religious services. Incorrigible monks were expelled from the abbey. Every monk had two coats, two cowls, a table-book, a knife, a needle, and a handkerchief, and his bed-furniture consisted of a mat, a blanket, a rug, and a pillow.

One of the most remarkable events of Glastonbury was the introduction of a German monk, Savaricus, as abbot. This was one of the stipulations for the release of Richard I. from his captivity in the castle of Dürrenstein on the Danube. The abbot Henry Swansea had to be superseded, and a violent opposition was made by the monks; but Swansea was made bishop of Winchester, and thus the storm was somewhat appeased, but its effects continued long. This was a proof that its wealth was so notorious as to excite the cupidity of even foreign monarchs. At the time of its fall the revenues of the abbey amounted to £200,000 per annum, according to the prefent value of money. The commiffioners of Henry VIII. thus defcribe its domains :—" The houfe of Glaftonbury is great, goodly, and fo princely that we have not feen the like. It has four parks adjoining : the furthermoft but four miles diftant from the houfe, having a large weir or lake, which is five miles in compafs, that being a mile and a half diftant from the houfe, well replenifhed with great pike, bream, perch, and roach. Alfo four fair manor places belonging to the lord abbot, the furthermoft three miles diftant, being goodly manfions, and alfo one in Dorfetfhire, twenty miles diftant from the monaftery." Whenever the abbot wifhed to go to one of thefe retreats, or elfewhere, he was accompanied by a retinue truly regal, confifting of a bannered hoft of a hundred or more in number, in fplendid military coftume, armed, and preceded by a great crucifix. The people thronged to the highway as he paffed, to receive his bleffing and pay him homage on their knees. In this ftyle he went up to parliament, where he fate mitred and croziered, the firft abbot of the realm.

In the laft abbot, Richard Whiting, Henry VIII. found a fturdy refifter of his fpoliation. He refufed to obey the royal injunction to furrender. He declared that he held the truft from God, for the fervice of religion and of the poor, and he would not concede his functions to mortal command. He was fummoned to Wells, and the Oath of Supremacy put to him. He refufed to take it. The church-reforming king did not paufe at trifles. He had the abbot waylaid ; a confeffor was forced into his carriage, and he was bade to prepare for death. In vain did he fupplicate for a few days to take leave of his brethren and prepare his foul; he was dragged to the top of Tor-hill on a fledge, where he could not only look down on

Glaftonbury, and all his noble eftate, but over a magnificent expanfe of country one hundred and forty miles in circumference. There lay below him the beautiful Ifle of Avalonia; the Wyralle or Weary-all-hill, the Chalice-hill. In the midft of this auguft fcene, enough to make the moft heavenward heart feel a touch of lingering affection, he was barbaroufly hanged, with his treafurer, John Thorn, and his under-treafurer, Roger James, on the 14th of November, 1539. His head was placed on the gate of his abbey, and his four quarters fent to be expofed at Wells, Bath, Ilchefter, and Bridgewater. Such was the fate of the laft of fifty-nine abbots who had held the crozier at that famous fhrine for one thoufand one hundred and fourteen years.

Rapacious hands very soon not only ftripped its altar, and rifled its coffers and walls, but dafhed in its gorgeous windows, demolifhed its carved monuments, reft from its roof lead and timbers, knocked down its lofty columns, fhattered its fculptured capitals and niches, and built cottages or made roads with its ftones grey with centuries. In the words of William Lifle Bowles:—

>All is filent now! Silent the bell,
> That heard from yonder ivied turret high,
> Warned the cowled brother from his midnight cell.
>   Silent the vefper chant—the Litany,
>   Refponfive to the organ! Scattered lie
> The wrecks of the proud pile, mid arches grey:
> While hollow winds through mantling ivy figh;
> And even the mouldering fhrine is rent away,
> Where in his warrior weeds the Britifh Arthur lay!

Amongft the remains at Glaftonbury, which are now preferved with care, are fome fine arches of the nave of the great church, with the chapel of St. Jofeph at the weft end. The chapel is a beautiful object, its principal walls remaining, and teftifying by their round arches, and efpecially by the one richly ornamented receding portal, its Norman period. The portion which connected it with the portico which led to it is of the later pointed ftyle, or Early Englifh, as is the abbey church itfelf. The abbot's kitchen remains entire, and the tower of St. Michael's church on Tor-hill ftands a ftriking object far over the country. The church itfelf was overthrown by an earthquake in 1276. The abbot's barn on the right of the road leading to Pennard, is another remaining building; and in High-ftreet, Glaftonbury, ftands an old building fuppofed to be the court-houfe, or tribunal. The churches of St. Benedict and St. John were alfo connected with the abbey. Some traces of wall are alfo fhown as having belonged to the old hofpitium of the abbey: and at the foot of Tor-hill on the north fide ftill flows the chalybeate fpring, regarded as holy during the palmy days of the abbey, and long afterwards of great celebrity for its healing quality.

We may clofe this notice by a curious fact mentioned by the Rev. J. Williams.—In July, 1859, was fold in London, by auction, the Conventual Regifter and Cartulary of Glastonbury Abbey, in which was inferted a letter of Bifhop Tanner, ftating that he had refcued the volume from deftruction at a grocer's. It realized £141 15s.

Iona, or Icolmkill.

IT would be difficult to imagine a voyage of more intereſt,—whether we regard natural beauty, poetical imagery, or the intellectual attractions of a ſacred antiquity,—than to the venerable ruins of Iona, once the Chriſtian ſchool which diffuſed its cheering light over the barbarous tribes, not only of Great Britain, but of the European continent. We there tread the ground hallowed by the footſteps of thoſe Britiſh apoſtles who reſiſted the haughty ſpirit of Rome, and planted the pure doctrines of the croſs in England, France, Germany, Switzerland, and even Italy. Columb and Columbanus, Gallus and Aidan, and others, who, purſuing the ſame work as their countrymen, Virgilius, Albin, Erigena, Clement, Donatus, etc., ſpread the independent Chriſtian truth far and wide in the face of domineering Rome.

In proceeding to this ancient Weſtern fane, which combines ſo many circumſtances which ought to be ever dear to Proteſtantiſm, we embark on a voyage of wild beauty, bringing us alſo into immediate communion with poetry as well as religion. As we have ſaid on a former occaſion, the ſpirit of Collins and Thomſon, of Oſſian, of Leyden, and Scott and Campbell, is upon us. We deſire to ſee the regions which they have inveſted with ſo many charms—to tread the lands of second-sight and airy spirits. We would look on the tombs and shattered images that stood when

> Aodh, famed afar,
> In Iona preached the word with power;
> And Reullura, beauty's star,
> Was the partner of his bower.

These words of Campbell's reveal to us that his Aodh lived when Rome had not asserted her dogma to the clergy, "forbidding to marry;" but the lonely Culdee, the missionary of these then semi-savage isles, had the comfort and society of his helpmeet to cheer him in his labours and sympathize in his discouragements and successes. Besides sailing for the region of these primitive labours, we are at the same time bound for the regions of ghosts and fays, of mermaids and kelpies, of great krakens, and a hundred other marvels and miracles. We sail along the busy banks of the Clyde, the romantic kyles of Bute, the cloudy heights and hollows of Arran; skirting the solitary shores of Cowal, and cutting through the Mull of Cantire by the Crinan canal, we issue into the Sound of Jura, and are in the swell of the wild Atlantic, surrounded by leaping waves and screaming sea-fowl, and dark storm-beaten crags. Soon we hear the roar, and observe the foaming waves, of the far-famed eddy of the Corywrekan, tossing and leaping in strange commotion. From Oban we set sail for the Western Isles, and as we traverse the Sound of Mull, behold, a thousand mountain-heights and objects whose names recall scenes of old romance. The castle of Duart, Artornish Hall, the cloudy land of Morven, the region of Ossian, and then we are in Mull, sailing up the very harbour of Tobermory, where one of the ships of the Spanish Armada perished. Then we are coursing over the breezy waters, amid distant prospects of the Hebrides, Eig, and Canna and Rum, and the blue tops of the far mountains of Skye, gazing on the near shores of Treshanish,

Gometra, Colonſa, and Mull; with Staffa, and its celebrated cave, a huge, iſolated crag, riſing from the waters before you.

IONA.

And anon you approach the rocky iſle of Icolmkill, a wild and naked crag-land of about three miles long and one wide. "It is needleſs," ſays Robert Chambers in his "Pictures of Scotland," to inform the reader that this is, as Johnſon expreſſes it, "the illuſtrious iſland, which was once the luminary of the Caledonian regions, whence ſavage clans and roving barbarians derived the benefits of knowledge, and the bleſſings of religion."—That it was, in the ſixth century, the place where Columbus, an Iriſh ſaint, firſt propagated the Chriſtian faith amongſt a people formerly devoted to the ſuperſtitions of Druidical paganiſm.—That it was for centuries the ordinary burial-place of the Scottiſh kings; and that it afterwards became at once an abbacy and the ſeat of the biſhopric of the Iſles. The relics which ſtill exiſt to atteſt its former greatneſs are very numerous. The cathedral is a building ſtill pretty entire, one hundred and ſixty feet long without, and thirty-four broad. Within the choir, which is itſelf ſixty feet in length, are ſeveral fine pillars, carved in the Gothic way with great variety of fanciful and ludicrous figures, repreſenting parts of ſcripture. Amongſt the reſt is an angel with a pair of ſcales weighing ſouls, and the devil keeping down that in which the weight lies with his foot. On his face is portrayed a malicious grin. The eaſt window is a beautiful ſpecimen of Gothic workmanſhip. In the middle of the cathedral riſes a ſquare tower of about eighty feet high, ſupported by four arches, and ornamented with bas-reliefs. In the chancel there is a tomb of black marble, with a fine recumbent figure of abbot Macfingone, who died in 1580. On the other ſide of the chancel is a ſimilar monument to the abbot Kenneth. On the floor is the figure of an armed knight, with an animal ſprawling at his feet. On the right of the cathedral, and contiguous to it, are the remains of the college, ſome of the cloiſters of which are ſtill viſible. The common hall is entire, with ſtone ſeats for the diſputants. A little to the north of the cathedral are the remains of the biſhop's houſe, and on the ſouth is the chapel dedicated to St. Oran, pretty nearly entire, ſixty feet long and twenty-two broad, but nearly filled with rubbiſh and monumental ſtones. In the encloſures adjoining to this building, forty-eight Scottiſh kings, four kings of Ireland, eight Norwegian monarchs, and one of France, are ſaid to be interred—perhaps the moſt extenſive holy alliance or congreſs of European ſovereigns on the other ſide of the grave. Icolmkill, which is properly termed Hii, and claffically Iona, was the depofitory of a vaft collection of valuable papers and books, all of which were difperfed or deftroyed at the Reformation. Other buildings of a monaftic character can be traced throughout the ifland.

Martin in his account of the Weftern Ifles, fays that Columba built two churches and two monafteries, one for men and one for women.—That in an empty piece of ground betwixt the church and the gardens, murderers and children who had not received baptifm were buried.—That near the weft end of the church, in a little cell, but without any infcription, is the tomb of Columba.—That a little further to the weft lie the black ftones on which Macdonald, king of the Ifles, delivered the rights of their lands to his vaffals in the ifles and continent, with uplifted hands and bended knees; and in this pofture, before many witneffes, he folemnly fwore never to recall thofe rights; and this was inftead of his great feal. Hence it was that when any one was certain of what he affirmed, he faid pofitively "I have freedom to fwear this matter upon the black ftones." At fome diftance from the cathedral is St. Oran's Church, commonly called *Reliqui Ouran*, becaufe the faint of that name is buried in it. About a quarter of a mile further is the church of Ronad, in which the prioreffes were buried.

Much deftruction of thefe remains has taken place fince Martin vifited the place, and much had been perpetrated before. It is faid that there were formerly three hundred and fixty ftone croffes in the Ifland of Iona, which fince the reformation have been reduced to two, and the fragments of two others. The fynod of Argyle is reported to have caufed no lefs than fixty of them to be thrown into the fea at one time; and fragments of others, which were knocked to pieces, are to be seen here and there, some of them now converted into grave-stones. Amongst the most curious sculptures remaining, are Adam and Eve eating the forbidden fruit under the tree, on St. Martin's crofs, which is eight feet high, composed of the red granite of the island, as are also the carved pavement of St. Oran's chapel, especially that of some singular bells, and the grotesque scenes carved on the capitals of the pillars in the cathedral.

The destruction here, in which the original erections of the Primitive British church have suffered for being found in connection with the additions of their Romish successors, are greatly to be regretted, especially when we observe the masterly style of the sculpture, the singular stories indicated in some of the carving on the walls, and the unique and beautiful foliage and flowers with which the tombs are adorned by the chisel, which cannot be seen without a lively admiration. No time of itself could have destroyed them; for they are mostly of the red granite, or syenite, of which the rocks and islets around consist; and are enclosed by low walls of the same stone, rounded into great pebbles by the sea.

The wild and desolate aspect of the place strongly impress on the visitor the perils and persecutions of those savage times, which drove the professors of the Christian faith to such a stony wilderness, amid the howlings of these northern seas. The present inhabitants of the island are exceedingly poor and ignorant. As you draw near the coast, you behold a low bleak shore, backed by naked hills, and at their feet a row of miserable Highland huts: and at separate intervals the ruins of the monastery and church of Ronad, the church of St. Oran and its burying-ground, and lastly, the cathedral raises its square, red, solemn bulk. You are immediately on landing surrounded by little children offering pebbles of green serpentine, which they collect on the shore, in little dishes: and by the guide offering his little books descriptive of the place and its antiquities. Every few days through the summer the steamer lands its passengers to view the ruins; but these bring no advantage to the place, for they make their survey, and then proceed on their voyage.

But from the present desolation the mind ascends back with an affectionate interest to that time when, from the sixth to the tenth centuries, the professors of the ancient Christian church of Britain and Ireland flourished here, guarded by the elements and the stern sterility of these then remote regions— "far off amid the melancholy main," and sent forth their devoted disciples to preach Christ, not only over the British isles, but on the continent. To those who would inform themselves of this noble race of preachers of a pure and primitive faith, we would recommend the perusal of a most interesting little volume entitled, — "Annotations on Dr. D'Aubigné's Sketch of the Early British Church," by Mrs. Webb of Dublin.* In this ably and earnestly written little volume Mrs. Webb has most completely demonstrated the error of Dr. D'Aubigné, in attributing the labours of this church to the Scotch instead of the Irish. To none but a foreigner could the name of Scots at that period have been supposed to refer to natives of Scotland. The Scots were natives of Ireland, who carried their name to Scotland, by migrating to the Highlands, the inhabitants of which are their descendants. Up to the eleventh century, Scotland bore the name of Albin, or Alba, latinized to Albania. "Irish and Ireland," justly remarks Mrs. Webb, "Scotch and Scotland, as at present applied, were introduced by the Normans in the eleventh century. Hibernia and Scotia, prior to that

* Published by Wertheim and Macintosh, Paternoster-row; A. W. Bennett, Bishopsgate-street; Robertson, Dublin; and Paton and Ritchie, Edinburgh.

date, were exclufively applied to the prefent Ireland, and fhould have been fo tranflated from the original of Bede's hiftory." Bede ufed the term Scot and Scotia as they were ufed in his day, Irifh and Ireland being names unknown.

We fhall not quote further proofs of the correctnefs of our authorefs's ftatement; they are too obvious to be denied. We fhall rather avail ourfelves of her facts, to fhow how noble a place was once Iona.

After the firft preaching of Chriftianity in Britain, and during thofe centuries in which Rome was overrun by the northern barbarians, the pagan Saxons perfecuted and expelled the Chriftian teachers from England. Charlemagne converted the Saxons on the Elbe by the perfuafive arguments of fire and fword to a nominal Chriftianity: but the pagan Saxons, who made themfelves mafters of England, murdered the Chriftian natives, and gave them no alternative but apoftacy or death. Numbers of thefe efcaped into Ireland. Mrs. Webb claims for the Irifh the enjoyment of letters from a period much anterior, and that they accepted thefe fugitive apoftles of Chrift's faith, "which was pure from any admixture of Roman elements, either of fophiftry or luxury, with open arms. And foon they fent forth a purer development of unfophifticated, practical Chriftianity, than had iffued from any of the old regions of Roman dominion. Hibernia's induftrious, felf-fupporting fchools, produced the principal Chriftian luminaries that irradiated the gloom of the continental nations between the fifth and eleventh centuries. During that period her indefatigable miffionaries, with their fimple habits and fingle-hearted devotion, fpread a knowledge of the gofpel and a tafte for letters among the Englifh Saxons, the Picts of North Britain, the Franks of Gaul, the inhabitants of Switzerland, and the Scandinavians of Iceland. Flanders, Germany, and even Italy herfelf, in thofe ages, were indebted to Hibernia for their moft accomplifhed teachers. And finally, ere the ecclefiaftical ambition of Rome, leagued with Norman love of power and plunder, had crufhed the independence of the Hibernian church, fhe had imprefled the phafe of gofpel principles on the dwellers in the mountains of the Vofges, the Alps, and the Apennines, where they ftill live amid much poverty and godly fincerity."

In afferting the general juftice of Mrs. Webb's ftatements, we muft at the fame time remark, that, like all zealous advocates, fhe has gone a little into the extreme. In defending the church of Ireland fhe has overlooked the primitive church of Wales, etc. : in maintaining the Bangor of Ireland fhe has ignored the Welfh Bangor. But the truth is, that when the Chriftians of England were perfecuted by the invading Saxons and Danes, they fled to Wales, Cornwall, and Armorica, as well as to Ireland; and great numbers remained there till finally crufhed by the church of Rome. Bangor in Wales, as well as Bangor in Ireland, was a great fchool of that church. We know that after the arrival of St. Auguftine from Rome in 597, with the forty monks fent by Gregory I., the fyftem of aggreffion on the Britifh church was perfiftently carried on till it was finally overpowered. We know that Ethelfrid, the king of Northumberland, the obedient inftrument of Auguftine, killed two thoufand of the Britifh clergy in cold blood at Caerleon, or Chefter. Neither muft we admit, what Mrs. Webb feems to infer, that the apoftles of Ireland firft planted the truth amongft the Waldenfes, Vaudois, etc. That truth exifted there from the apoftolic times, and would make them welcome fuch men as Columba, Gall, and Clement, who there ftrengthened but did not originate thofe churches.

But too much praife cannot be beftowed on thefe Irifh and Iona miffionaries for what they did. St. Patrick appears to have been the son of one of those British Christians who had taken refuge in Brittany, and who being, as a youth, carried off by Irish pirates to Ireland, became there the great means of spreading Christianity amongst the wild tribes of that island. A great school of Christianity was established at Bangor in the county Down, which sent out many famous and indefatigable men. One of these was St. Columb, who went over and settled on the barren island of Iona in the year 565, thirty-two years before the arrival of St. Augustine in England. There, with some of his Christian companions, he built an humble abode and an humble church. Columb was a member of the Royal family of Ireland, a grandson of Fergus, and his original name was Crimthan; but the name of Columba, or the Dove, was given him on account of his meekness. Amid this stormy ocean they established a seminary of Christian education, Columba maintaining the most simple life, and having a stone for his pillow. "The sages of Iona," says D'Aubigné, "knew nothing of transubstantiation, or the withdrawal of the cup in the Lord's Supper, or of auricular confession, or of the prayers to the dead, or tapers, or incense; they celebrated Easter on a different day from Rome. Synodal assemblies regulated the affairs of the church, and the Papal supremacy was unknown. The sun of the gospel shone upon these wild and distant shores. In after years, it was the privilege of Great Britain to recover with purer lustre the same sun and the same gospel." St. Columb and his companions and followers at Iona were the great missionaries of the Christian faith amongst the Picts of Scotland.

From the same primitive school, bearing their independence boldly against Rome, went forth from Iona and Bangor a noble host. Columbanus, a younger and different man from Columb, went forth with his friend Gall into Switzerland and France. They established Christian schools in the Vosges, and founded the abbey of Luxeuil. There they had numbers of zealous ftudents. Twenty years afterwards, Columbanus being expelled from the Vofges, Gall fettled in Switzerland; but Columbanus proceeded to Lombardy, and there, under the patronage of the king, Agilulf, founded the convent of Bobbio in the Apennines. The fchools in the Vofges remained, and Columbanus was invited to return to them; but he declined, and continued to live at Bobbio with his friend Jonas the abbot. St. Gall founded the monaftery called after him, and of which the town ftill retains the name, on the river Steinach, and died at the age of ninety-five.

Aidan, an apoftle from the ifland of Hii, or Iona, was invited by Ofwald, king of Northumberland, to Chriftianize his people, amongft whom he laboured affiduoufly, travelling everywhere on foot, and giving everything that he had to the poor amongft whom he preached. He became firft bifhop of Lindisfarne, where he died in 651, twenty-two years before the birth of Bede, venerated to enthufiafm by the people. His fucceffors, Finan and Colman, had to ftand ftrong contefts with the abbot Wilfrid, and the reft of the Roman clergy, and were finally compelled to return to Iona. But from the Hibernian fchool went forth other miffionaries, extending their field of labour to the continent. Clement fpread the gofpel in Bavaria, where, protefting againft the errors of Rome, he was denounced and fent prifoner to the Pope. The Catholic clergy were efpecially fcandalized at his being a married man. Fellow-labourers of his were Sampfon and Virgilius. The latter carried the gofpel into Carinthia, and became bifhop of Saltzburg, but not without encountering the hoftility of the papal clergy whofe errors he oppofed. So far was Virgilius before his age, that he anticipated Galileo, and declared that there were antipodes,—a theory much difcuffed even in the third century, and ridiculed by Lactantius. For this Virgilius was denounced as a heretic by Boniface, the archbifhop of the German churches.

Another of thefe Irifh miffionaries in the ninth century, John Scotus Erigena, fettled at the court of Charles the Bald, translated the works of Dionyfius the Areopagite, and, what was ftill more extraordinary, in his work, "Margarita Philofophiæ," firft broached the fyftem of phrenology, revived by Gall a thoufand years afterwards, either with or without the knowledge of Erigena's theory. In a copy of this work depofited in the libraries of Oxford or Cambridge, it is faid that the human fkull is mapped out into different organs, fimilar to thofe of Gall.

Another of thefe extraordinary men, Claude Clement, more commonly called Claude or Claudius of Turin, in the ninth century founded the Univerfity of Paris; and his friend John Scott, called Albinus, founded that of Pavia. Claude became bifhop of Turin, where he lived till the year 839, forty-feven years after he quitted Ireland, having had to maintain an arduous conflict with Rome againft its errors, the worfhip of images, the interceffion of faints, etc. "If thofe," he faid, "who have forfaken idols, worfhip the images of the faints, then they have not forfaken idols, but changed their names. Whether thou painteft thy walls with figures of St. Peter and St. Paul, or of Jupiter and Saturn, neither are the latter gods, nor the former apoftles." Claude's countrymen, Sedulius, became bifhop of Oreta, and Donatus of Fiefole; and modern travellers have been aftonifhed amid the valleys of the Vaud to hear airs of Scottifh pfalmody, which had no doubt been planted there by thefe early apoftles of Britain.

Calling to mind the memory of this early race of devoted men, members of the ifland church of Iona, or of the mother of Iona, Bangor, we tread the defolate ftones of thefe ruined fhrines with an exalted pleafure. From this wafte fea-wildernefs what feeds of the great truth have been sown wide over the earth, now producing a hundred and a thousand-fold in the restored church, under its modern name of Protestantism.

Poetry has delighted to hang its wreaths on the shattered columns of Iona. Collins says :—

> Where beneath the showery west,
> The mighty kings of three fair realms were laid :
> Once foes, perhaps, together now they rest ;
> No slaves revere them, and no woes invade.
> Yet frequent now, at midnight's solemn hour,
> The rifled mounds their yawning cells unfold,
> And forth the monarchs stalk with sovereign power,
> In pageant robes and wreathed in shining gold,
> And on their twilight tombs aërial council hold.

But Campbell has sung a nobler strain in honour of " the dark-attired Culdee," for so were the clergy of Iona called. He represents an invasion of Iona by a band of savage Danes, who ravage the place, but are surprised by the apparition of St. Columbkille, who destroys their leader by causing the fall of his statue upon him, and sends them astonished away. All this Reullura, the wife of the Culdee Aodh, had foretold; but she herself has, during the onset of the Danes, plunged into the sea and perished.

> Star of the morn and eve
>   Reullura shone like thee,
> And well for her might Aodh grieve,
>   The dark-attired Culdee.
>
> Peace to their shades! the pure Culdees
>   Were Albyn's earliest priests of God,
> Ere yet an island of her seas
>   By foot of Saxon monk was trode ;
> Long ere her churchmen by bigotry
> Were barred from holy wedlock's tie.
> 'Twas then that Aodh, famed afar,
>   In Iona preached the word with power ;
> And Reullura, beauty's star,
>   Was the partner of his bower.

But, Aodh, the roof lies low,
  And the thistle-down waves bleaching,
And the bat flits to and fro,
  Where the Gael once heard thy preaching:
And fallen is each columned aisle
  Where the chiefs and the people knelt.
'Twas near that temple's goodly pile
  That honoured of men they dwelt.
For Aodh was wise in the sacred law,
  And bright Reullura's eyes oft saw
The veil of fate uplifted.
Alas, with what visions of awe
  Her soul in that hour was gifted!

When the saint had confounded the marauders by his presence, and destroyed their chief—

A remnant was called together,
A doleful remnant of the Gael,
And the Saint in the ship that had brought him hither
  Took the mourners to Innisfail.*
Unscathed they left Iona's strand,
  When the opal morn first flushed the sky,
For the Norse dropped spear, and bow, and brand,
  And looked on them silently.
Safe from their hiding-places came
Orphans and mothers, child and dame:
But alas! when the search for Reullura spread
  No answering voice was given,
For the sea had gone over her lovely head,
  And her spirit was in heaven.

And so the catastrophe of the venerable Iona was complete; the mourners returned to Innisfail, and the church and the schools of the Culdees remained desolate till made the seat of a papal abbacy.

                    * Ireland.

Lanthony Abbey.

ANTHONY ABBEY, in the retired vale of Ewias, in Monmouthſhire, preſents in its remaining ruins one of the fineſt ſpecimens of the Norman-Gothic. It was built in the year 1108, in the reign of Henry I., when the Norman rule, and the Norman taſte in everything, prevailed. All who have ſeen the Abbaye aux Hommes and Abbaye aux Dames at Caen, in Normandy, built by William the Conqueror and by Matilda his queen, will be at once ſtruck by the reſemblance, eſpecially in the ſquareneſs and maſſiveneſs of the outlines, and of the ample and ſquare towers. In theſe fine old remains we have that mingling of the round arches of the paſt Saxon and the pointed ones then firſt introduced. The pointed arches, too, are of differing characters; ſome are acutely lancet, others of a more obtuſe faſhion. The building is divided at every ſeparate height of window by bands running along the whole façade; and the weſt front in particular exhibits thoſe unions of arches, and alſo blank arches, which marked the progreſs of Anglo-Gothic from the ſingle round arches of the old Saxon, into a greater freedom, airineſs and ornament. The northern ſide has the leaſt mixture of the Norman pointed arch, and in the eaſt are immenſe entrance arches of both kinds.

LANTHONY ABBEY.

Lanthony, like Glaſtonbury and many other monaſteries, had its literary monk, who became its hiſtorian; and from the monk of Lanthony we learn the following particulars, as preſerved by Dugdale in his "Monaſticon:"—St. David, uncle of king Arthur, finding a ſolitary place amongſt woods, rocks, and valleys, built a ſmall chapel on the banks of the Honddy, or Black Water; pronounced Honthy. He paſſed many years in this hermitage, but after his death it was deſerted for ſeveral centuries. It ſtill, however, retained the name of Lan Dewi Nant Honddu, or the church of St. David on the Honddy, ſince corrupted into Lanthony. But its reſtoration was by one William, a military retainer of Hugh de Laci, a great Norman baron of the reign of William Rufus, who, whilst hunting, suddenly discovered the mouldering hermitage of St. David, and was struck by a desire to abandon the world, and finish his days there. "He dismissed his companions," says the monk of Lanthony, "and devoted himself to God. He laid aside his belt, and girded himself with a rope; instead of fine linen he covered himself with hair-cloth, and instead of his soldier's robe he loaded himself with weighty irons. The suit of armour, which before defended him from the darts of his enemies, he still wore as a garment to harden him against the soft temptations of his old enemy, Satan, that, as the outward man was afflicted by austerity, the inner man might be secured to the service of God. That his zeal might not cool, he thus crucified himself, and continued his hard armour on his body until it was worn out with rust and age."

He was afterwards joined by Ernesti, the chaplain of Maud, the queen of Henry I., and they built a small chapel in 1108. This was soon afterwards augmented by Hugh de Laci, earl of Hereford, the patron of William, into a priory of canons regular of the order of St. Augustine. Large gifts of money and land were soon offered, but the two brethren declined them, desiring to "dwell poor in the house of God;" and they were so earnest in defence of their poverty, that they put up constant public prayers against wealth, and deprecated its acquisition as a dreadful misfortune. But their pious resolution, like that of all other monks, was speedily overcome by the arts of a woman. "Queen Maud," says the monk of Lanthony, "not sufficiently acquainted with the sanctity and disinterestedness of William, once desired permission to put her hand into his bosom, and when he, with great modesty, submitted to her importunity, she conveyed a large purse of gold between his coarse shirt and iron boddice, and thus, by a pleasant and innocent fubtlety, adminiftered fome comfortable relief to him. But oh! the wonderful contempt of the world! He difplayed a rare example that the trueft happinefs confifts in little or nothing! He complied, indeed, but unwillingly, and only with a view that the queen might employ her devout liberality in adorning the church."

But the charm was broken; gold had found its way into the priory, and by its inevitable attraction abundance more flowed after it. Splendid buildings fpeedily arofe, and in the midft of them a magnificent church. For a while fomething of the priftine difcipline continued, however, and the monk of Lanthony defcribes the place and eftablifhment in thefe terms:—" There ftands in a deep valley a conventual church, fituated to promote true religion, beyond almoft all the churches in England: quiet for contemplation, and retired for converfation with the Almighty. Here the forrowful complaints of the oppreffed do not difquiet; the mad contentions of the froward do not difturb: but a calm peace and perfect charity invite to holy religion, and banifh difcord. But why do I defcribe the fituation of the place, when all things are fo much changed fince its priftine eftablifhment? The broken rocks were traverfed by herds of wild and fwift-footed animals; thefe rocks furrounded and darkened the valley, for they were crowned by tall towering trees, which yielded a delightful profpect at a great diftance to all beholders, both by fea and land. The middle of the valley, although clothed with wood, and funk in a narrow and deep abyfs, was fometimes difturbed by a ftrong blighting wind; at other times obfcured with dark clouds and violent rains, incommoded with fevere frofts, or heaped up with fnow; whilft in other places, there was a mild and gentle air. The large and plentiful fprings from the neighbouring mountains fell with a pleafant murmur into a river in the midft of the valley, abounding with fifh. Sometimes, after great rains, which were extremely frequent, the floods, impatient of conftraint, inundated the neighbouring places, overturning rocks, and tearing up trees by the roots. Thefe fpacious mountains, however, contained fruitful paftures, and rich meadows for feeding cattle, which compenfated for the barrennefs of other parts, and made amends for the want of corn. The air, though thick, was healthful, and preferved the inhabitants to an extreme old age; but the people were favage, without religion, vagabonds, and addicted to ftealth. They had no fettled abode, and removed as wind and weather inclined them."

This is a fufficiently lively defcription of a location amid Welfh mountains at that period. The monks were doomed to feel the effects of the civil ftrife betwixt Maud and Stephen. The Welfh took refuge in the convent, and, in fact, feem to have taken free poffeffion of it. They came with their wives and children, and quartered themfelves in every part of it. The women took poffeffion of the refectory. They fang profane fongs, and fcandalized the holy brethren " by their light and effeminate behaviour." Complaining of this rude invafion to Robert de Betun, bifhop of Hereford, he invited the monks to Hereford, and then prevailed on Milo de Laci to grant them ground at Hyde, near Gloucefter, where they built a church in 1136. But this proved the ruin of Lanthony. The monks were too much attached to the populous and more civilized city, and refufed to return to the old Lanthony when the troubles were over. The new Lanthony, as the Gloucefter eftablifhment was called, received ample endowments from King John and other benefactors. The monks were courted by the great, and foon revelled in every fpecies of luxury and worldly pride. They claimed the pre-eminence of the new over the old monaftery.

"When the ftorm fubfided," fays the monk of Lanthony,

" then did the fons of Lanthony tear up the bounds of their mother church, and refufe to ferve God as their duty required: for they faid there was much difference between the city of Gloucefter and the wild rocks of Hatyrel; between the river Severn and the brook of Hodani; between the wealthy Englifh and the beggarly Welfh—*there* fertile meadows, here barren heaths. Wherefore, elated with the luxuries of their new fituation, and weary of this, they ftigmatifed it as a place unfit for a reafonable creature, much lefs for religious perfons. I have heard it affirmed, and I partly believe it, that fome of them declared in their light difcourfe,—I hope it did not proceed from the rancour of their hearts,—that they wifhed every ftone of this ancient foundation a ftout hare. Others have facrilegioufly faid,—and with their permiffion I will proclaim it,—they wifhed the church and all its offices funk to the bottom of the fea. They have ufurped and lavifhed all the revenues of the church; *there* they have built lofty and ftately offices; *here* they have fuffered our venerable buildings to fall to ruin. And to avoid the fcandal of deferting an ancient monaftery, long accuftomed to religious worfhip, and endowed with large poffeffions, they fend hither their old and ufelefs members, who can be neither profitable to themfelves nor others, who might fay with the apoftle, We are made the fcum and outcaft of the brethren. They permitted the monaftery to be reduced to fuch poverty, that the friars were without furplices, and compelled to perform the duties of the church, againft the cuftom and rules of the order. Sometimes they had no breeches, and could not attend divine fervice; fometimes one day's bread muft ferve for two, whilft the monks of Gloucefter enjoyed fuperfluities. Our remonftrances either excited their anger or ridicule, but produced no alteration: if thefe complaints were repeated, they replied—" Who would go and fing to the wolves? Do the whelps of wolves delight in loud mufic? They even made fport, and when any perfon was fent hither, would afk, 'What fault has he committed? Why is he fent to prifon?' Thus was the miftrefs and mother-houfe called a dungeon and a place of banifhment for criminals."

The old Lanthony never furmounted thefe ufurpations of the new. Its library was defpoiled of its books; its ftorehoufe of its deeds and charters; of its filk veftments and relics, embroidered with gold and filver; and the treafury of its precious goods. Whatever was valuable or ornamental in the church of St. John was conveyed to Gloucefter, without the fmalleft oppofition, and at laft the Gloucefter monks carried thither its very bells, notwithftanding their great weight. Edward IV. made the Gloucefter Lanthony the principal, but compelled the monks to maintain a prior and four canons at the original abbey. At the diffolution in 1539 the old Lanthony was valued at £71 3s. 2d., and the Gloucefter monaftery at £648 19s. 11d. At that period Richard Hempfted was the prior of Lanthony, and on his furrender he obtained a penfion of £100 a-year. Anthony à Wood fays that he carried away many ancient manufcripts from the abbey, and gave them to his brother-in-law. The abbey was fold to one Richard Arnold, and was purchafed of Arnold's defcendant, Captain Arnold of Lanvihavel, by Harley the minifter of Queen Anne, and fo became the property of the Earls of Oxford.

In 1806 Lanthony was purchafed by Walter Savage Landor, the celebrated poet and profe writer. For the eftates of Lanthony and Comjoy he paid in purchafe-money and improvements £70,000. His improvements were extenfive. He for many years employed between twenty and thirty labourers in building and planting. He made a road at his own expenfe eight miles long, and planted and fenced half a million of trees, and had a million more trees ready to plant. But Lanthony was not deftined to become more agreeable to him than it had been to the monks. According to his own ftatement to us, he received fuch infamous treatment from both his fteward and his principal farmers, during his fojourn on the continent, that he determined to abandon the place as a refidence. He had built a houfe at a coft of £8,000, but he pulled it down ftick and ftone, that his fon might not be expofed to fimilar vexations by living there. Two farmers efpecially, brothers, whofe united rents amounted to £1,500 per annum, refufed all payment till compelled by law, and then fled to America. From thefe tenants the fteward received £1000; but Landor fays he never faw a farthing of the money, and he was afterwards obliged to difmifs the fteward too. He ftates that he had twelve thoufand acres of land at Lanthony, much of it, of courfe, mountain; and that he had twenty watchers of game on the hills night and day, but that he never faw a groufe upon his table, though the game coft him more annually than he lived at after leaving Lanthony.

Such is the hiftory of one of the fineft monaftic ruins in one of the moft monaftic feclufions of the United Kingdom. Thofe who now vifit it will find part of the priory buildings converted into a fmall romantic inn: and, whilft they contemplate the profound repofe of its fituation, will little fufpect the paffions and difcontent which have agitated and embittered its hiftory from the days of William and Ernefti to thofe of the impulfive author of " Ghebir" and " Imaginary Converfations."

Near the ruins of the abbey there is a fubterranean paffage, faced with hewn ftone, about four feet fix inches high. The people fay that, according to tradition, it paffes under the mountains to Oldcaftle, which, if it were true, would connect it with another place of great intereft—the houfe of Sir John Oldcaftle, Lord Cobham, the leader of the Lollards in the reign of Henry V., who concealed himfelf at this Oldcaftle for fome time, but was taken and burned in St. Giles's Fields in 1417; being, fays Horace Walpole, " the firft author, as well as the firft martyr, amongft our nobility."

LANTHONY.

There may be mightier ruins;—Conway's flood
   Mirrors a mafs more noble far than thine,
And Aberyftwith's gaunt remains have ftood
   The ceafelefs fhock where wind and wave combine;
Lone is Dolbadarn, and the lovely fhrine
Of Valle-Crucis is a fpell of power,
   That ftills each meaner thought and keeps enchained;
Proud of that long army of arch and tower,
   Raglan may claim a rude pre-eminence;
Tintern is peerlefs at the moonlit hour,
   Neath, Chepftow, Goodriche, each hath its pretence;—
But mid thy folitary mountains, gained
   By no plain beaten path, my fpirit turns
To thee, Lanthony! and, as yet untrained,
   Freely to worfhip in thy precinct yearns,—
Now, left to nature's Pilgrims unprofaned!

Chepstow Castle.

EARS ago, as I iffued from the Briftol fteamer, and was afcending the fteep High-ftreet of Chepftow, on a fine autumn morning, I became aware of a tall, ftout, florid-looking man in middle life, alfo labouring up behind me. There was a crowd of other paffengers who had defcended from the fame fteam-boat, and were afcending the fame ftreet,—fome before me, fome behind me,—but I became, fomehow, particularly confcious of the following of the large, ftout man. There was his heavy, meafured tread, always at a certain diftance in my rear, which I neither left farther aftern by quickening my pace, nor put a-head by flackening it, and this it was that, no doubt, foon made me efpecially fenfitive to this ponderous fequitur. If I have a fidgetty averfion to one thing more than another, it is to have fomething pad, padding at my heels, like the Fakenham ghoft. I often ftop fhort to let a cart, or a carriage of any kind, that is going on grinding and jarring befide me, or a perfon who comes tramp, tramp, with an inceffant, unvarying ftep, clofe behind me, go its, his, or her way. But this coloffal humanity was not thus to be got rid of. To accelerate or leffen my fpeed only produced the fame effect on my follower: there might have been a rod or bar of fome kind fufpended betwixt us, and regulating our diftance. As no graduation of progreffion availed to remove the incubus, I fuddenly ftopped and directed

my attention into a fhop window; the huge man as fuddenly did the fame. I gave a fide-glance at him, but he appeared to be profoundly contemplating a pair of bellows of no particular novelty of fafhion. I fprang forward as abruptly as I had ftopped, hoping that my great fhadow was fufficiently attracted by the bellows to adhere, and thereby, like the fhadow of Peter Schlemyhl, fall away from me. Nothing of the kind. As if my removal was the inevitable caufe of his, he turned gravely and renewed—his chafe?—no; his purfuit?—no, it could not be faid to be either, but his mechanical following. But he is fat, I thought; and thereupon I put, to ufe a Derbyfhire phrafe, my beft leg foremoft, and went up the fteepeft part of the ftreet at a rate of at leaft five miles an hour. It was ufelefs. The ftupendous man, if he were not the actual grey man of Peter Schlemyhl, had on, it feemed, his feven-league boots. With enormous ftrides and the equally great accompanying ftretches of a ftout ftick, he cleared the pavement wonderfully, and was ftill juft two yards behind me.

"This is intolerable!" I faid to myfelf, and, wheeling fuddenly round, I ftood and gazed down over the town, and over the Wye circling round its bafe, and over the Gloucefterfhire fields and woods beyond. The man wheeled round too, blew a large hot breath from his puffed cheeks—I had tired him a little then!—took off a capacious broad-brimmed hat, and, wiping a capacious forehead with a brilliant red and yellow filk handkerchief, revealed a gigantic head—what a head he had!—covered with a profufion of brown and curly hair.

"A very fine view," he obferved, ftill gazing round on the extenfive fcene of town and fhips, and Wye and diftant Severn. "Very!" I faid, fomewhat fhort. "Very, indeed," he replied with a much more amiable complacency. I went on, and fo did the imperturbable, inevitable ftranger. Then thought I, if he will ſtick to me, here he ſhall ſtand ſome time and cool his heels. I ſtood ſtill and ſtared him full in the face. He looked with a broad, frank look,—I could not call it a ſtare —alſo at me, and obſerved, "I take it you are for the Beaufort Arms?" "I am," I reſponded. "Then I am for the Beaufort Arms, too." It was too much: I went on again, and as the great ſtranger entered the lobby of the houſe at the ſame moment, he obſerved, "I take it that you propoſe to breakfaſt here?" "Juſt ſo," I replied. "Then I am for breakfaſt, too," he added ; "and ſo we may as well breakfaſt together."

The adheſive tendency of the ſtranger was ſingular, but he had nothing ſiniſter or unpleaſant in his appearance; I was under no apprehenſion of bailiffs or ſpies, nor did he look like either; on the contrary, he had an ample, open, good-natured and intelligent aſpect. There was nothing to be ſaid againſt his propoſition. I ſate down to a table ready ſpread, and ordered coffee and beefſteak. "The ſame for me," ſaid the incomprehenſible, and ſeated himſelf oppoſite to me. We breakfaſted for ſome time in ſilence, then the great preſence began to drop ſententious remarks: the air in the early morning in the boat was chilly—the ſun now was very cheering— this town ſtood on a very ſteep hill-ſide—a good inn this Beaufort Arms—and ſo on; to all which I aſſented, for there was no denying the aſſertions.

We paid our bills, and roſe ſimultaneouſly. "And now, I take it," ſaid my choſen companion,—the choice being all on his inſcrutable ſide,—"that you are for Tintern." "Exactly so," I ſaid. "Then I am for Tintern, too," he remarked, "and ſo let us join at a chaiſe, or a boat. I don't mind which."

"But firſt," I ſaid, "*I* ſhall viſit the caſtle here." "By all means," he replied; "I am at your ſervice for that."

"And so," I thought, as we began to descend again to the left towards the castle ruins, " my jolly Great Unknown, you are for Tintern,—six miles, and a good spell up-hill; and you dream of a boat up the Wye, or a chaise up the steep here—ha! ha! we shall see! I now perceive a coming divorce from my zealously attached one. If he *will* do as I do on the way to Tintern, I warrant him he never did such a penance yet; so, whatever the upshot, let us at all events be agreeable. A chaise indeed! A boat!"

I must in my internal amusement have said the last words audibly, for my great rosy friend remarked, " Ay, it will be a boat, I think, for we are descending." At the next moment we stood before that great extent of ancient towers and walls, enclosed in their grass-grown ditch, and beautifully draped with ivy. I pulled out my guide-book; my great double, or rather quadruple, drew out one exactly the same. " What an extensive place," I observed, and began to read; my friend—for I think I may call him so, for he showed a remarkable preference for my company—also reading in silence. " The castle was founded in the eleventh century by William Fitzosborn, Earl of Hereford, a relative of William the Conqueror. In the thirteenth century the greater part of the original structure was taken down, and one, larger and of great strength, was erected. It is still a magnificent pile, towering upon the summit of a cliff whose base is washed by the classic Wye. The site occupies three acres of ground, and is divided into four courts." " That is probable," I observed,—"I mean, that it arose in the eleventh and thirteenth centuries, for it bears a wonderful resemblance to the old castle and town-walls of Conway, which were built in the eleventh. You observe these great round battlemented towers, with their straight battlemented walls, ftretching from one tower to the other." "I never faw Conway," replied my friend; "that is interefting."

But we need not repeat all our remarks. I will now awhile draw from more extenfive fources than the guide-book the chief particulars of the hiftory of this caftle. There have not been wanting thofe who have attributed the original

CHEPSTOW CASTLE.

ftructure to the Romans, fimply becaufe a few Roman bricks are vifible in the walls of what is called the chapel. It may have been fo; but the Britons at leaft had a caftle here, which they called Caftell Gwent, or Cafgwent, as the town was called by the Saxons Chepeftowe, or place of trade. But the

Normans, who raifed what remains now, termed it Striguil, and it appears in Doomfday-Book as Caftellum de Eftrighoiel, and in ancient charters is named Striogul, Striguil, etc. It is divided into four courts, two of which are now ufed as gardens. As you enter the great eaftern portal you behold on your right hand a number of dilapidated offices, befides the lodge of the keeper, and on your left hand the fouth-eaftern ancient tower or citadel, now called Marten's Tower. On your left hand in the third court ftand the walls of a fine old gothic building, ninety feet in length, and thirty in breadth, which is called the chapel, but was probably the baronial hall. The ftyle of the arches and niches which remain are more modern than the reft of the caftle, and poffefs much elegance. The fourth court was approached formerly by a drawbridge, long ago deftroyed; and the entrance at the weftern extremity of the caftle was alfo defended by a portcullis, and another drawbridge over the ditch.

The William Fitzofborn who built Striguil or Chepftow caftle, fought, it feems, at Haftings, and in reward for his fervices was made jufticiary of England, and received this property, as well as others. But it did not remain in his family beyond the next generation. His eldeft fon, like nearly all the Normans who came with the Conqueror who had eftates at home, returned to them, and left landlefs adventurers to get eftates in England. His fecond fon was a monk; and his third fon, Roger, rebelled againft the king, and was put in prifon. Whilft there the king fent him a fuit of royal robes,—that is, a fuit of his caft-off clothes,—which fo offended him that he threw them into the fire. This, again, fo incenfed the king that he vowed, "by the brightnefs of God," that the proud Roger fhould never come out of prifon; and there Roger died. The king then gave his eftate to Gilbert, furnamed Strongbow, brother of

Richard, Earl of Clare. The original name of this Strongbow was Tonnebruge, a name which shows his Danish origin, Dannebrog being the great Danish standard. This Richard Tonnebruge, therefore, was doubtless descended from a stout northman, the standard-bearer of the Dannebrog, when the northmen seized Normandy. In the Norman transmigration the name had been corrupted into Tonnebruge, and in England soon became further corrupted into Strongbow. These Strongbows were fine fellows. Richard, the grandson of the original Richard, conquered Ireland, and married the daughter of Dermot, king of Leinster, and held Dublin, making over, however, his conquests to king Henry II. of England. His daughter Isabella married William, Marshal of England, and founded the illustrious family of the Earls of Pembroke. The husband of Isabel Strongbow, the first Earl of Pembroke, was one of the greatest men that England has produced. Dugdale says of him,—" This illustrious peer was the greatest warrior in a period of warfare, and the most loyal subject in an age of rebellion: by the united influence of wisdom and valour he supported the tottering crown of king John, broke the confederacy of the barons, who had sworn allegiance to Louis, dauphin of France, drove away the foreign usurper, fixed Henry III. on the throne of his ancestors, and gave peace to his distracted country."

And all this is most true. For though it has suited our historians to go on affirming and re-affirming the tale that the barons won the Magna Charta from king John at Runnymede; and though, like parrots, we go on talking of "the barons of Runnymede," and of their winning Magna Charta; the truth is that they never did win Magna Charta, and that the charter of king John never was our Magna Charta, but the charter of Henry III. True, the barons *forced* John to sign a charter at Runnymede, but John well knew that, by all the laws of nations, a thing obtained by force is not a valid thing: therefore, no sooner was the charter signed than he repudiated it: and the barons, knowing quite as well that a *forced* contract thus repudiated was no contract at all, took up arms to compel him again to acknowledge their charter. But, so far from this, John, backed by the brave Earl of Pembroke, resisted, and beat the barons at every point. What then did these same much-lauded barons? They did a most shameful and unpatriotic deed. They offered the crown of England to Louis, dauphin of France, which, had he obtained it, would have reduced this country for ever to a mere province of France. But John beat both the barons and their king Louis of France: and when John died, there was found in his pocket, says Carte the historian, a letter signed by forty of these barons, offering to resign all question of the charter, if he would restore them again to their titles and estates. Neither living nor dying, however, did John do this, but treated the barons as traitors.

When he was dead, the brave seamen of Dover, putting Hugh de Burgh at their head, and the brave archers of England, putting William de Collingham at their head, determined to settle the matter with the barons, and drive away their French king. At this time Louis and the barons held London and the south of England, and were powerfully supported by the King of Scots in the north, and the Prince of Wales in the west; but the freemen of England, the sailors and archers, beat them all, and compelled the Dauphin to flee into his ships at the mouth of the Thames. They destroyed all his ships except fifteen, with which he got him away. And then, these freemen of England having saved England from a *French* as well as a Norman invasion, marched up to London, and com-

pelled the king to grant them a new and better charter than
that of John. The king, Henry III., was but a boy of ten
years old, but this brave Earl of Pembroke was his guar-
dian and regent of the kingdom, and by his advice Henry
granted a new charter, containing a new claufe, ordering the
demolition of every caftle built or rebuilt during the wars of
the barons. This charter was not now figned in the prefence
of the king and the barons only, but in that of the king and
the united parliament; for the reprefentatives of the burghs
are expreffly mentioned as fitting in the parliament of 1265.
Befides the Great Charter, the people now demanded and
obtained the Charter of the Foreft—a mighty boon, by which
all the forefts enclofed fince the days of Henry II. were
thrown open, and the deadly foreft laws were deprived of
their bloody and capital power. This is the true ftory of the
Great Charter of England, as related by Matthew Paris,
Rhymer, Carte, and other hiftorians, not won by rebellious and
traitorous barons, who would have fold us for ever to France,
but by the people of England themfelves, who fhould not allow
themfelves to be lightly defrauded of their glory. This is what
Dugdale means by faying that the brave Pembroke "broke
the confederacy of the barons, who had fworn allegiance to
Louis, dauphin of France, and drove away the foreign
ufurper." The great men of Dugdale's time knew what was
our true hiftory, and would not allow it to be falfified: and
Blackftone in his "Commentaries," and in his "Effay on
Magna Charta" fully fubftantiates thefe great facts, and fays
that the charter of John never was our charter, but the far
better charter of Henry III.;—that we had other and better
charters than John's, both before and after his time, and that his
charter, which never became the charter of the realm, would
never have been heard of but for his war againft the barons.

My ſtout and inſeparable friend was greatly amazed at this revelation that the charter of Runnymede was of no more value than a bill drawn on a party who diſhonours it; but I ſaid, " Think of that and talk of that at home, but now call to mind that extraordinary men have been priſoners within theſe walls. Here the good and learned biſhop, Jeremy Taylor, was incarcerated in 1656, on a charge of being privy to an inſurrection of the royaliſts. And here," I ſaid, " in the ſouth-eaſtern extremity of the firſt court, you ſee the tower ſtill called Henry Marten's Tower, where Marten, one of the regicides, was confined. This was one of the moſt determined republicans of his time. He was the friend of Harrington, Sydney, Wildman, Neville, and other men who had imbibed all the republican ideas of ancient Greece and Rome. He it was who, walking between the Parliament Houſe and Weſtminſter with Mr. Hyde, afterwards the famous Lord Chancellor Clarendon, long before the civil war, ſtartled him by ſaying, "*I do not think one man wiſe enough to govern us all!*" He was the right-hand man of Cromwell, till Cromwell himſelf aimed at ſovereign power. He it was who, when the high court of juſtice appointed to try Charles I. were puzzled on what authority they ſhould try him, roſe and ſaid, " In the names of the commons and parliament aſſembled, and of all the good people of England." And when Charles himſelf demanded on what authority they preſumed to try him, he was anſwered in thoſe words. He would have been executed with the reſt of the regicides, but for his latter oppoſition to Cromwell. On that account his puniſhment was commuted to perpetual impriſonment.

Marten was a priſoner in this tower twenty years, but his impriſonment was by no means rigorous. His wife was permitted to reſide with him; he had the full enjoyment of his property, which was large, and was allowed to receive visits, and to pay visits, in company with a guard, to the neighbouring gentry, especially to a Mr. H. Pierre, at whose house a fine portrait of him was preserved.

CHEPSTOW, MARTEN'S TOWER.

Southey in his early and democratic poems drew a most gloomy and exaggerated picture of Marten's imprisonment here :—

>For *thirty* years *secluded* from mankind,
>Here Marten lingered. Often have these walls
>Echoed his footsteps, as with even tread
>He paced around his *prison*. Not to him
>Did Nature's fair varieties exist—
>He never saw the sun's delightful beams;
>Save when through yon high bars he poured a sad
>And broken splendour.

The Rev. Mr. Coxe visiting this castle in 1800, and having in his mind this doleful description, was, he says, greatly "surprised to find a comfortable suite of rooms. The first story contained an apartment which was occupied in his time by Marten and his wife; and above were the lodgings of his domestics. The chamber in which he usually lived was not less than thirty-six feet in length and twenty-three in breadth, and of proportionate height. It was provided with two fireplaces and three windows, two of which appeared to be the original apertures, and the third was probably enlarged for Marten's convenience!"

A circumstance at which the public was greatly scandalized at the time, was, that when the judges who had tried Charles I. signed the warrant for his execution, Cromwell, taking up the pen to sign, daubed the face of Henry Marten, who sat next him, with the ink; and Marten, when the pen was handed to him, returned the same compliment to Cromwell. Something of this levity continued to show itself in Marten, who lived to the age of eighty-seven. His epitaph, written by himself, may yet be seen in Chepstow church, and is curious, forming an anagram on his name.

HERE,
September 9, in the year of our Lord, 1680,
   Was buried a true Englishman
   Who in Berkshire was well known
   To love his country's freedom 'bove his own:
   But living immured full twenty year
   Had time to write, as doth appear,

HIS EPITAPH.
H ere or elsewhere, (all's one to you, to me,)
E arth, air, or water gripes my ghostless dust,
N o one knows how soon to be by fire set free.
R eader, if you an oft-tried rule will trust,
Y ou'll gladly do and suffer what you must.

M y life was spent with serving you, and you,
A nd death's my pay (it seems,) and welcome too :
R evenge destroying but itself, while I
T o birds of prey leave my old cage and fly.
E xamples preach to the eye ; care then—mine says—
N ot how you end, but how you spend your days.

Having taken a view over the walls of the castle court, and at the Wye rushing far below at the base of the cliffs on which the castle stands, we set out for Tintern.

Tintern Abbey.

"AND now for Tintern!" I said to my stout friend. "Ay, ay! for Tintern!" he replied gaily: "but first, my dear sir, for a boat." "For a boat! why we are a full mile from the bridge. It would be a loss of time to go all the way down for a boat." "Well, then, let it be a chaise." "First," I said, "let us have a peep in at the gates of Piercefield. It is just above here, and we can see it better and with more time than with a chaise waiting for us." So, though with a dubious and misgiving air, my friend moved on with me. The ascent of the Monmouth road was pretty steep, but I endeavoured to beguile his attention by talking of Piercefield. "This Piercefield," I observed, "is one of the paradises of England. Here we are: we will take the liberty of just walking inside the lodge-gate—it is a show-place; they won't object. There! see what a charming spot! What a delightful stretch of woods and lawns, and park-like fields! What views out beyond! If we had time to traverse these celebrated scenes—to view the majestic Wynd Cliff and the Bannagor Rocks opposite, and the bold peninsular of Lancaut, all towering magnificently above the Wye—to visit the Lover's Leap, and traverse the woods that skirt the river deep below, and take in all the varying views of dizzy heights and sylvan dells—you would wonder that any one ever left this place. Yet it has in not very many years paſſed through many hands. One of its various poſſeſſors was the generous Valentine Morris, governor of St. Vincent, in the Weſt Indies, who firſt comprehended the beauty of the ſpot, and opened it up, by walks and drives, to the feet and the eye

VIEW FROM CHAPEL HILL.

of the lover of nature. Poor Morris!—imprudent as benevolent, and treated with the groſſeſt diſhoneſty by a baſe government, he was as unfortunate as he was philanthropic; yet you will find his memory retained lovingly in Chepſtow.

"And here, too, it is pleaſant to think that that good and gifted young woman, Elizabeth Smith, whom the laſt genera-

tion knew and admired, paſſed the chief part of her ſhort life. Her father bought this place when ſhe was eight years old, and, as ſhe died about twenty years after, here ſhe muſt have gathered up all that ſtore of languages which ſhe chiefly taught herſelf, with the exception of the two firſt:—French, Italian, Spaniſh, German, Latin, Greek, Hebrew, Syriac, Arabic, and Perſian. Elizabeth was one of the firſt to make England acquainted with the wealth of German literature, particularly with 'Klopſtock.' Little is known of her now; but ſhe deſerves to be remembered, were it only for one ſentence occurring in her letters:—' To be good and diſagreeable is high treaſon againſt virtue.'"

As I was talking of theſe things, I had quietly quitted the park of Piercefield, and we were again mounting the ſteep road. Suddenly my companion exclaimed, "But where are we going? This is not the way for the chaiſe!" "Nonſenſe about chaiſes," I ſaid; "Don't you ſee that we are now far on the way to Tintern? We ſhall be preſently at the Wynd Cliff, one of the fineſt views you ever ſaw; we are better without a chaiſe, or any other bother." "Ha!"—ſaid the large man, "You are drawing me on! I ſee it—I ſee it. But no! it won't do. Why, to walk all the way to Tintern would kill me!" "All the way to Tintern I ſuppoſe is now about four miles," I replied; "and that can do you no harm, ſurely." "No harm! Why, ſir, I have never for theſe twenty years walked four miles at a ſtretch. With my weight, my good ſtout horſe, or my carriage and pair of greys, are much pleaſanter. I never walk further than round my grounds, or to my factory and back." "So, you are a manufacturer?" and he then informed me that he was a cotton-ſpinner of Derbyſhire. "Of Derby-ſhire! why then we are countymen. And now look here. By not walking you make yourſelf heavy, and loſe one of the finest enjoyments of life. Here am I, older than you are, and I have just walked from Falmouth to the Land's End, and from the Land's End to Barnstaple, with many a goodly zigzag besides, here and there, in Cornwall; and as for a chaise, I should be ashamed to put my foot in one for such a mere stride. To be candid, I won't have anything to do with a chaise, and so I suppose here we must part."

"Astounding!" said the great man, for he was evidently given to wonder—" and you've really done that, and are all the better for it. But no; it may do for you, but it would not do for me. I could not think of it!" "Then good-bye," said I, extending my hand: "I thought we were just going to make a pleasant county acquaintance." He stood as taken quite aback. "Well, I had set my mind on going to Tintern with you, I don't know why—but four miles yet!" "Four fiddlesticks!" I said: "Come along, it will do you good, and we might have been half-way there now." He shook his head; but suddenly he said, "And you really think it will do me good?" "I do." "Then here goes," he said; and on we marched, with a good hearty "Bravo!" on my part.

It was a stout climb to the Wynd Cliff, and my worthy and robust cotton-spinner perspired freely, and wiped his ample brow industriously, and exclaimed, "This is very severe; but it *may* do me good." Anon we stood on that splendid height the summit of the Wynd Cliff: and as my neophyte in peripatetics gazed down on the Wye far below, rushing with the inflowing tide between its lofty rocks, and then glanced on the scenes around, he burst forth with an emphatic "Glorious!"

"You are right," I said; "but button up your waistcoat and your coat, for the wind is cool here, and I will read you from the guide-book all the objects you can see from this spot."

"The extenfive profpect commanded from this fummit is generally extolled as one of the moft beautiful in the ifland. The objects included are,—the new line of road from Chepftow to Tintern; the Wye winding in its circuitous courfe between its rocky and wooded banks; the pretty hamlet of Lancaut, with the perpendicular cliffs of Bannagor, and the whole domain of Piercefield; a little to the left Berkeley Caftle and Thornbury Church. On the right fucceffively the caftle and town of Chepftow; the majeftic Severn, and the confluences of the rivers Wye and Severn; the Old and New Paffages; Durdham Down, and Dundry Tower, near Briftol; the mouth of the Avon and Portifhead Point: to the fouth-weft, the Holmes and Penarth Point, near Cardiff: and far away in the north-weft the Black Mountains, forming a fublime background to the whole: thus embracing parts of nine counties, namely, Monmouth, Gloucefter, Wilts, Somerfet, Devon, Glamorgan, Brecon, Hereford, and Worcefter. In the words of Mr. Rofcoe—'The grouping of the landfcape is perfect: I know of no picture more beautiful.'"

My great friend refted in full enjoyment of this magnificent fcene—*refted*, that made no fmall part of the charm, for he had found a feat. He would have dwelt on each point, and endeavoured by queftions to identify every one of them; but I reminded him that he might take cold, and we proceeded on our way. But the great difficulty was now paffed—the reft of the road was pretty level, and I endeavoured to keep up his attention by pointing out the beauties of the ftrangely-circling Wye to our right. I told him of the advantages people drew from walking; of the acquaintance it gave them with the people paffing the fame way, or as you fat awhile with them in their cottages. "Ay," faid he, eagerly looking round, "that fitting in a cottage muft be pleafant;" but there was no cottage vifible. And I went on telling him of the many poems Wordfworth wrote from materials picked up in walking, or on the top of coaches—(" I prefer the top of coaches, myfelf," faid he.)—that Wordfworth at Goodrich Caftle thus met with the little girl who gave him the idea of " We are Seven ;" and alfo walking along the Wye from Builth to Hay, he fell in with " Peter Bell." The countenance, gait, and figure of Peter, he tells us, were taken from a wild rover with whom he walked from Builth, and who told him ftrange ftories. I then drew from my pocket the fmall Paris edition of Wordfworth's Poems. " This book," I faid, " gave great vexation to Wordfworth ; for when he had not made fifty pounds in his whole life by the fale of his Englifh edition, this pirated one had fold one hundred and twenty thoufand copies in Paris. It annoyed him, but it will pleafe us." And I began to read his

"LINES WRITTEN ON REVISITING TINTERN."

Five years have paft; five fummers, with the length
Of five long winters! And again I hear
Thefe waters, rolling from their mountain-fprings
With a fweet inland murmur.—Once again
Do I behold thefe fteep and lofty cliffs,
That on a wild fecluded fcene imprefs
Thoughts of more deep feclufion ; and conneƈt
The landfcape with the quiet of the fky.
The day is come when I again repofe
Here, under this dark fycamore, and view
Thefe plots of cottage ground, thefe orchard tufts,
Which at this feafon, with their unripe fruit,
Are clad in one green hue, and lofe themfelves
Among the woods and copfes, nor difturb
The wild green landfcape. Once again I fee
Thefe hedge-rows, hardly hedge-rows, little lines
Of fportive wood run wild ; thefe paftoral farms
Green to the very door; and wreaths of fmoke
Sent up, in filence, from among the trees!
With fome uncertain notice, as might feem,
Of vagrant dwellers in the houfelefs woods,

Or of some hermit's cave, where by his fire
The hermit sits alone.
    These beauteous forms,
Through a long absence, have not been to me
As is a landscape to a blind man's eye :
But oft, in lonely rooms, and 'mid the din
Of towns and cities, have I owed to them,
In hours of weariness, sensations sweet,
Felt in the blood, and felt along the heart ;
And passing even into my purer mind
With tranquil restoration :—feelings too
Of unremembered pleasure : such, perhaps,
As have no slight or trivial influence
On that best portion of a good man's life,
His little nameless, unremembered, acts
Of kindness and of love. Nor less, I trust,
To them I may have owed another gift,
Of aspect more sublime ; that blessed mood,
In which the burthen of the mystery,
In which the heavy and the weary weight
Of all this unintelligible world
Is lightened :—that serene and blessed mood,
In which the affections gently lead us on,—
Until, the breath of this corporeal frame
And even the motion of our human blood
Almost suspended, we are laid asleep
In body, and become a living soul :
While with an eye made quiet by the power
Of harmony, and the deep power of joy,
We see into the life of things.
      If this
Be but a vain belief, yet, oh ! how oft,
In darkness, and amid the many shapes
Of joyless daylight ; when the fretful stir
Unprofitable, and the fever of the world,
Have hung upon the beatings of my heart,
How oft, in spirit, have I turned to thee,
O sylvan Wye ! Thou wanderer thro' the woods,
How often has my spirit turned to thee !
And now, with gleams of half-extinguished thought,
With many recognitions dim and faint,
And somewhat of a sad perplexity,
The picture of the mind revives again :
While here I stand, not only with the sense

Of prefent pleafure, but with pleafing thoughts
That in this moment there is life and food
For future years. And fo I dare to hope,
Though changed, no doubt, from what I was when firft
I came among thefe hills; when like a roe
I bounded o'er the mountains, by the fides
Of the deep rivers, and the lonely ftreams,
Wherever nature led: more like a man
Flying from fomething that he dreads, than one
Who fought the thing he loved. For nature then
(The coarfer pleafures of my boyifh days,
And their glad animal movements all gone by,)
To me was all in all.—I cannot paint
What then I was. The founding cataract
Haunted me like a paffion: the tall rock,
The mountain, and the deep and gloomy wood,
Their colours and their forms, were then to me
An appetite: a feeling and a love,
That had no need of a remoter charm,
By thought fupplied, or any intereft
Unborrowed from the eye.—That time is paft,
And all its aching joys are now no more,
And all its dizzy raptures. Not for this
Faint I, nor mourn nor murmur; other gifts
Have followed, for fuch lofs I would believe
Abundant recompenfe. For I have learned
To look on nature, not as in the hour
Of thoughtlefs youth; but hearing oftentimes
The ftill, fad mufic of humanity,
Nor harfh nor grating, though of ample power
To chaften and fubdue. And I have felt
A prefence that difturbs me with the joy
Of elevated thoughts; a fenfe fublime
Of fomething far more deeply interfufed,
Whofe dwelling is the light of fetting funs,
And the round ocean and the living air,
And the blue fky, and in the mind of man:
A motion and a fpirit, that impels
All thinking things, all objects of all thought,
And rolls through all things. Therefore am I ftill
A lover of the meadows and the woods
And mountains: and of all that we behold
From this green earth; of all the mighty world
Of eye and ear, both what they half create

> And what perceive ; well pleafed to recognize,
> In nature and the language of the fenfe,
> The anchor of my pureft thoughts, the nurfe,
> The guide, the guardian of my heart and foul,
> Of all my moral being.

I read the whole, though we muft not quote the whole here. "And thefe," I faid, "are the pleafures that men, and women too, for the poet's fifter was with him, feize upon by quitting their lazy carriages, and entering on the fineft eftate which God and nature have given them, a vigorous pair of legs. Thefe are the fine free thoughts ranging through woods and mountains, and by pleafant rivers, when age or ficknefs or other neceffity fhall have cut off all travelling, fave in the enchanted regions of memory."

"It is very fine, very," faid the great manufacturer, "and I am fure it will do me a world of good; but it is very fevere" —and he wiped again his reeking brows, and flung open his ample waiftcoat. "But here we are! See, there are the gables of Tintern, its broken walls and arched windows rifing out of its wood of trees!" It was a fcene of quiet, truly monaftic beauty. The fmoke afcended in the clear autumnal air from the hamlet cottages near, and the Wye, now brim full from the height of the tide, gave a perfecting charm to the landfcape. We entered the interior of the beautiful ruin in filence. No one ever enters the place without being deeply impreffed by its noble proportions, and the claffical grace and chaftity of its architecture. This abbey church was built in 1131, and prefents a fine fpecimen of the early-Englifh ftyle, blending into a more ornamented character, as later additions were made or changes introduced. The roof is gone, but the walls are entire ; all the pillars, except thofe which divide the nave from the northern aifle, and the four lofty arches which fupporting the tower fpring high into the air, though reduced to narrow rims of ſtone, ſtill preſerve their original form. The weſtern window, with its rich tracery, is extremely beautiful. "From the length of the nave," ſays Coxe, "the height of the walls, the aſpiring form of the pointed arches, and the ſize of the eaſt window which cloſes the perſpective, the firſt impreſſions are thoſe of grandeur and ſublimity. But as theſe emotions ſubſide, and we deſcend from the contempla-

WEST DOOR AND WINDOW.

tion of the whole to the examination of the parts, we are no leſs ſtruck with the regularity of the plan, the lightneſs of the architecture, and the delicacy of the ornaments. We feel that elegance is its characteriſtic no leſs than grandeur, and that the whole is a combination of the beautiful and the fublime."

What Coxe alfo adds is true, and gives a peculiar beauty to the place. " Inftead of dilapidated fragments overfpread with weeds and choked with brambles, the floor is covered with a fmooth turf, which by keeping the original level of the church, exhibits the beauty of its proportions, and heightens the effect of the grey ftone. Ornamented fragments of the roof, remains of cornices and columns, rich pieces of fculpture, fepulchral ftones and mutilated figures of monks and heroes, whofe afhes repofe within thefe walls, are fcattered on the greenfward, and contraft prefent defolation with former fplendour."

My weighty friend feated himfelf on a tomb; but I, obferving an iron railing furrounding the top of the walls, looked for the afcent thither, and found that the walls were double, and that ftairs afcended between them. I foon, therefore, ftood aloft over my friend's head, and eagerly invited him to come up, and fee the charming view all around, and the admirable perfpective of the church below. " Not for the world!" he exclaimed—" Not for the world ! My legs have done wonders to-day, but my head would never ftand that." " Good," faid I. He had done wonders, and I had done one too ; for I had wiled him on to Tintern, fix good miles, and up a long, fteep hill, and now he *muſt* walk back. It was more than he had done for the laft twenty years.

The hiftory of Tintern contains nothing very remarkable. It was founded by the Strongbows, and became rich and hofpitable. Edward II. fought refuge there for fome time from the purfuit of his queen Ifabella. At the diffolution it contained only thirteen monks, and was valued with its eftates, according to Dugdale, at £132, but according to Speed at £256, per annum. It was granted by Henry VIII. to the fecond Earl of Worcefter, and is now the property of the Duke of Beaufort.

When we fet out to return, my companion, inftead of exhibiting fatigue, fprang up from his fepulchral feat, as he remarked, " like a giant refrefhed." He feemed infpired by a vivid fenfe of the feat that he had accomplifhed. " What would they fay at Chapel-en-Frith if they could fee me to-day! When I tell them that I walked to Tintern and back, eh? But I tell you what, my friend, I have been thinking of what you have faid as I fate on the tombftone there, and I think you are right. One grows fluggifh and ftupid by riding and lolling in carriages. I will walk! I feel lighter already: and I will be lighter ftill. Why fhould not I be as agile as you? You walked up Cornwall. I am going to Devonfhire, and I'll tramp it there as I'm alive!" And infpired by his new idea, the coloffal man really became a Coloffus of roads, for he ftrode along with a vigour, and with ftrides that required all my recent training on the moors and rocks of Cornwall to compete with him. He had found a new pleafure, a new power, and I had to warn him not to abufe it. " Ah!" faid he, " now I am putting you to your paces," and he ftalked on with a prodigious activity that aftonifhed me. Luckily it was downhill from the Wynd Cliff to the bridge at the bottom of Chepftow, where the fteamer lay, or I might have found myfelf worfted in the rapid walk with my elated companion. But it was all very well, for the bell was already ringing on the fteamer, and we had only time to rufh on board ere the plank was pulled back, and we were afloat. My ftout friend fat down with a laugh, but I rather think, neverthelefs, that he was glad the feat was ended, for he fat very perfiftently during the voyage. How little, when he had fingled me out for his companion to Tintern, *did* he know what a day might bring forth!

Raglan Castle.

> Not farre from thence, a famous caftle fine,
> That Raggland hight, ftands moated almoft round;
> Made of freeftone, upright and ftraight as line,
> Whofe workmanfhip in beauty doth abound,
> The curious knots, wrought alle with edged toole,
> The ftately tower, that looks o'er pond and poole,
> The fountain trim, that runs both day and night,
> Doth yield in fhowe, a rare and noble fight.—
>   Churchyard's *Worthines of Wales.*

RAGLAN CASTLE, as in its greater part it is one of the moft recent caftles in Monmouthfhire, fo it muft have been one of the moft fplendid as well as extenfive. The ruins, including the citadel, occupy a tract of ground one-third of a mile in circumference. As Churchyard ftates, who defcribes the ftately fabric as it ftood in all its glory in the reign of Elizabeth; it is built of a fine light-coloured freeftone which was fmoothly dreffed, and is beautifully grained. The ftone has received little injury from time; moft of the elaborately carved mafonry remains as fharp and diftinct as when firft executed; and from the parts which, except the roofs, remain entire, you receive a lively idea of its elegance and fplendour before it was difmantled by command of the parliament after furrendering to Sir Thomas Fairfax, and before its materials were plundered by the tenants to build houfes for themfelves. The foundations and remaining walls fhow it to have occupied an irregular square, enclosing two courts; the main residence, including the great hall and chapel, and other splendid apartments, running between these courts entirely from north to south. This interior portion of the castle appears to have been built in the reign of Queen Elizabeth, for it has all the characteristics of the architecture of her time, partaking more of the hall than the castle; its windows being chiefly square and mullioned, and each successive story divided by a running band. In the hall, or banqueting room, which is sixty feet long, and twenty-seven broad, you are struck with the gigantic size of the fire-place, and the singular structure of the

RAGLAN CASTLE.

chimney. At the upper end are the arms of the firſt marquis of Worceſter, ſculptured in ſtone, and ſurrounded with the garter, underneath which is the family motto :—" Mutare vel timere ſperno." —" I ſcorn to change or fear." The towers of the external buildings are generally ſquare, and not battlemented, but machicolated, ſo that their heads expand, and give them an air of firmneſs and grandeur. In the walls you can trace the changes of different periods, but the earlieſt ſtyle is not anterior to the reign of Henry V., and the lateſt comes down to that of Charles I. The main part of the caſtle probably was built by Sir William ap Thomas in the reigns of Henry V. and VI., and his ſon William Herbert, created by Edward IV. Earl of Pembroke, and Lord of Raglan, Chepſtow, and Gower, in 1469. From Dugdale's account it is ſcarcely poſſible to conceive in the preſent time the magnificence of the caſtle, and the greatneſs of the eſtabliſhment maintained in it by this Earl of Pembroke. Yet the vaſt extent of the ruins, the evident grandeur and number of the apartments, the ſize of the offices and the cellars, give proofs of baronial magnificence and ſplendid hoſpitality. In a curious account of the caſtle drawn up ſhortly before the parliamentary ſiege, and partly printed in Heath's account of Raglan Caſtle, the eſtabliſhment of its then proprietor, the firſt marquis of Worceſter, the numerous officers of his houſehold, retainers, attendants, and ſervants, appear like the retinue of a ſovereign rather than a ſubject. He ſupported for a conſiderable time a garriſon of eight hundred men; and, on the ſurrender of the caſtle, beſides his own family and friends, the officers alone were no leſs than four colonels, eighty-two captains, ſixteen lieutenants, ſix cornets, four enſigns, four quarter-maſters, and fifty-two eſquires and gentlemen. The demeſnes of the caſtle were of proportionate greatneſs: there were extenſive gardens and pleasure-grounds, extensive parks well stocked with deer, and numerous goodly farms. The two courts of the castle were surrounded by offices of all kinds, and the eastern court contained extensive barracks. This court was called the Fountain Court, from a marble fountain in the centre surmounted with the statue of a white horse; but of fountain or horse no traces now remain. On the south side of the castle stood the citadel, a large hexagonal fortress defended by bastions, and surrounded by a moat, over which passed a drawbridge from the castle. It was called Melyn y Gwent, or the yellow tower of Gwent, and when entire must have been a magnificent object, for it was five stories high. From this tower a vast prospect was enjoyed of the surrounding country, bounded by the distant mountains in the neighbourhood of Abergavenny. The citadel was surrounded by raised walks, in which Charles I., when staying here during his wars, took great delight. Great care has been taken since the restoration of the monarchy, by its owners, now the ducal family of Beaufort, to preserve the ruins; and the whole may yet be seen from some of the towers. The grand entrance is, perhaps, the most magnificent portion of these noble ruins. It is formed by a gothic portal, flanked by two massive towers, now beautifully hung with ivy. In the porch are still visible the grooves for two portcullisses; and the spectator on entering is greatly impressed by the scene. A guide lives in one of the towers, and the Duke of Beaufort has promoted the accommodation of visitors by keeping the paths and stairs in good order, and by placing seats for necessary rest.

The great point in the history of Raglan Castle is the defence it made against the parliament in favour of Charles I. By its strength and the spirit of its possessor, Henry Somerset, fifth earl and first marquis of Worcéster, the power of Charles was so long maintained in South Wales. It was nearly the

RAGLAN CASTLE, GRAND STAIRCASE.

laſt fortreſs in the kingdom that ſurrendered to the republican army. The traces of the outworks caſt up in front of the caſtle and citadel, are yet viſible in the remains of baſtions, hornworks, trenches, and ramparts. The marquis who made this ſtout defence,—after the army which he kept up of fifteen hundred foot and five hundred horſe under the command of his ſon, afterwards Earl of Glamorgan, was diſperſed by the parliamentary generals,—was a great wit, and his ſmart ſayings are preſerved in a work called "Witty Apothems of King James, Charles I., and the Marquis of Worceſter." Charles I. made ſeveral viſits here during his campaign againſt his ſubjects; but when he was compelled at length to retreat from Monmouthshire, the castle was invested by Trevor Williams and Colonel Morgan, and finally compelled to surrender by Fairfax himself. The marquis, and his son Glamorgan, are said to have lent to Charles I. at different times £300,000; and besides this they lost all their estates, valued at £20,000 a-year, which were confiscated; but restored on the return of Charles II.

The Strongbows seem to have been amongst the earliest possessors of Raglan. Richard Strongbow, the last male of the great family of Clare, according to Dugdale, conferred this property on Walter Bloet, or Blewitt, from whom by marriage it went into the Berkeley family, and so continued till it came into the possession of Sir John Morley, and, by Maud his daughter and sole heirefs, into the family of the Ap Jenkins, *alias* Herberts, in 1438. Edward IV. commanded William, whom he created Lord of Raglan, Chepstow and Gower, to continue the family name as Herbert, and not to change the surname at every descent in the Welsh fashion. To the custody of this Lord Herbert he entrusted Henry, Earl of Richmond, afterwards Henry VII., and he kept him in this his castle of Raglan till Jasper, then Earl of Pembroke, the uncle of this Lord Herbert, in his absence enabled Henry to escape, and fled with him to Britany. Edward IV. then attainted Jasper, and conferred the earldom on Lord Herbert. This is the same Earl of Pembroke that Wordsworth mentions in the " White Doe of Rylston," as having his head struck off in the porch of Banbury church, by one of the Cliffords. This Earl of Pembroke, being a staunch Yorkist, was defeated and taken prisoner at the battle of Dane's Moor, where he headed a band of his Welshmen. His sole heirefs married Sir Charles Somerset, a natural son of Henry Beaufort, Duke of Somerset, but in high favour with Henry VII., and from him his estate and titles have descended to the present Duke of Beaufort.

The family produced fome remarkable men. This Sir Charles Somerfet, who, though illegitimate, defcended from John of Gaunt, was a man of great perfonal attractions, and equal prudence and ability. Prudence and ability were precifely the qualities to recommend him to Henry VII., by whom he was employed in various foreign embaffies. He was equally in favour with Henry VIII., and had a high command in the wars againft France. He negotiated the peace with France in 1518, and the peace betwixt Francis I. and Charles V. in 1521. He reprefented Henry VIII. at the coronation of the king's fifter Mary, the queen of Louis XII. of France; and betrothed Henry's infant daughter Mary to the Dauphin. We have already mentioned Henry the fifth earl and firft marquis of Worcefter—his determined partizanfhip of Charles I.—his defence of Raglan, and his "Apothems;" one of which was uttered when Charles fhowed, as he thought, too much lenity to his enemies:—"Well, fir, you may chance to gain you the kingdom of heaven by fuch doings as thefe, but if ever you get the kingdom of England by fuch wayes I will be your bondman." The old man was a ftout Catholic; his eftates were confifcated, and, contrary to the conditions of his furrender, he was committed to the cuftody of the Black Rod. When told, however, that he would be allowed burial in his family vault at Windfor, he exclaimed:—" Why, God blefs us all, then I fhall have a better caftle when I am dead, than they took from me when I was alive !" He died at the age of eighty-five.

The fon of this Henry was Edward, the fixth earl and fecond marquis of Worcefter, who was created by Charles I. Earl of Glamorgan. Like his father, he was a firm Catholic. This was the Glamorgan who was engaged by Charles I. to bring over ten thoufand Irifh to enable him to crufh the liberties of England. The fcheme failed ; he was arrefted, by the Marquis of Ormond and Lord Digby; and Charles haftened to difavow the conduct of Glamorgan, though nothing is better afcertained than that he acted wholly in concert with the king. The tranfaction gave immenfe difguft in England, and did the greateft mifchief to Charles; even his ftaunch adherent, Clarendon, denouncing it in ftrong terms. Glamorgan followed the fortunes of Charles II., and being fent to England on his concerns in 1652, he was difcovered and imprifoned. To obtain his liberation he offered to make important difcoveries to Cromwell: and thefe after fome hefitation were accepted. His fon, who had hitherto lived in France, was permitted to return, enjoyed the confidence of Cromwell, and a penfion of £2,000 per annum.

This was the famous Marquis of Worcefter who wrote and publifhed, in 1663, " A Century of the Names and Scantlings of fuch Inventions as I can at prefent call to mind to have tried and perfected." Horace Walpole fneers at this book, little dreaming what was to come out of it, and dubbed it " A lift of a hundred projects, moft of them impoffibilities." One which the clever biographer of " Noble Authors" would doubtlefs have confidered the moft impoffible of all was the fteam-engine, and in its train all our prefent great fteam and railway fyftems. But in this work of the marquis was the following defcription of a fire-engine, in the fixty-eighth article of the " Century of Scantlings :"—" An admirable and forcible way to drive up water by fire, not by drawing or fucking it up, for that muft be, as the philofopher calleth it, *intra fphæram activitatis*, which is loft at fuch a diftance. But this way hath no boundary if the veffels be ftrong enough," etc. He then goes on to defcribe how he has forced water up a ftrong cylinder forty feet high, and how he could keep up the action by admitting cold water by a couple of cocks, fo that as the water in one was being confumed, it could be fupplied firft by one cock, and then by the other, etc.

This certainly was not the firft time the idea of exercifing force by fteam had occurred; for Gibbon, in his " Decline and Fall," relates how the architect of St. Sophia in Conftantinople avenged himfelf of the annoyances of his next neighbour, a lawyer, by running pipes up his houfe-fide, and introducing them under his roof, and continually fhaking the houfe over his head by explofions of fteam. Neither does it appear that the idea was an original fuggeftion of the marquis's own mind or experiments, but that in Paris he had feen the unfortunate Solomon de Caus, who was confined in the Bicêtre as a lunatic, for afferting the wonders that might be done with fteam. We are afraid that the marquis, being of an experimental turn, liftened to the poor man's fuppofed lunacy, and on his return to England made a number of experiments at his houfe at Lambeth, and boafted much of the wondrous power of his fire-engine. But if the marquis did not do proper honour to De Caus, he was deftined to receive the fame treatment. According to the "Experimental Philofophy" of Defaguliers, a Captain Savary bought up all the books of the marquis that he could lay his hands on, burnt them, and ftarted the idea as his own. In confequence of the number of the marquis's "Century of Scantlings" deftroyed by Savary, the book is very rare, but the contents of it may be found in the eighteenth volume of the "Gentleman's Magazine." Thus from Raglan iffued, if not the origination of the marvellous agency of fteam, the great revolutionizer of the world, at leaft the revival of it.

Conway and its Castle.

HE ancient walled town of Conway, with its picturefque caftle, ftands as the portal to the mountain fcenery of North Wales. Its fituation is beautiful, on high ground, commanding the eftuary of the Conway, whence its Welfh name of Aber-Conway; and its form triangular, or rather that of a Welfh harp. It was ftrongly fortified with walls and battlemented towers, according to the ftyle introduced by the Crufaders; and indeed Conway, with its walls, as feen at the prefent day from fome of its neighbouring heights, is faid greatly to refemble Jerufalem. The caftle, one of the moft picturefque ruins in England, was erected by Edward I. to keep the infubordinate Welfh in fubjection, and was completed under his own infpection in 1284. It was at the abbey of Conway that the head of the unfortunate but brave Prince Llewellyn was prefented to the Englifh conqueror. It is feldom that the name of the architect of any of our fine old buildings remains connected with them to pofterity; however, in the cafe of Conway, we find it to be Henry de Elreton, the builder likewife of the caftle of Carnarvon.

In its perfect ftate Conway Caftle was a magnificent ftructure, oblong in form, and ftanding on a precipitous rock at one corner of the triangular town-walls. On one fide it was bounded by the river, on another by a creek filled with each returning tide, and the other two faced the town. It was moated on the land fide and reached by a drawbridge, whilft a fmall fortified entrance communicated with the river by a narrow flight of fteps. The walls, which were of great thicknefs, were flanked by eight circular embattled towers, each furmounted by a flender watch-tower, which add great beauty of detail even to the outline of the ruins. On each fide of the grand entrance was a tower, the King's and the Queen's Towers, as they were called, and in each a beautiful oriel window. Two large courts occupied the interior. The great hall was one hundred and thirty feet long, by thirty-two wide, and was thirty feet high, lighted by nine fine lancet-formed windows, fix facing the country, and three looking into the court. The roof was fupported by eight maffive arches, four of which ftill remain, now garlanded with ivy. This fplendid apartment was warmed by three fire-places, and the eaftern end was partitioned off as a chapel, lighted by a large window. Beneath this hall were the vaults for ammunition and ftores.

Conway was a military ftation and free borough, its inhabitants being Englifh, and enjoying "many privileges;" one of which was that "the Jews dwell not at any time in the faid borough." In 1290, the Welfh having rifen in rebellion, hanged the royal collector of taxes, and routed the Englifh troops, whereupon the king marched into North Wales, and, croffing the eftuary with his guards, took up his quarters in the caftle, but not without great lofs of baggage and ftore wagons, which were intercepted by the mountaineers, who came down in great numbers and invefted the caftle. The rifing of the river at the fame time prevented the troops from croffing, fo that the king was reduced to great ftraits, and, like his garrifon, was obliged to content himself with salt meat and coarse bread, and to drink water sweetened with honey. At length the waters subsiding, the troops crossed, and the Welsh dispersed to their mountains. The Christmas of that same year was spent by Edward and his queen with great festivity at the new castle of Conway.

Eleven years afterwards, Edward of Carnarvon, the first Prince of Wales, held a court at Conway, when Einion, Bishop of Bangor, and David, Abbot of Maenon, near Llanrwst, did homage; and, on ascending the throne, this Edward still further increased the privileges of the burgesses.

In 1399, Conway was the scene of one of the last acts in the tragedy of the unfortunate Richard II. An account of this event has been preserved in a narrative, in rude verse, preserved in the library of the British Museum, entitled "An Account of the Treachery of the Earl of Northumberland, and the taking of his Majesty Richard II., his progress from Conway to Rhuddlan, Flint, and Chester. By an Eye-witness." This curious and interesting old document, which formerly belonged to Charles of Anjou, Earl of Maine and Mortaine, was translated into English prose, in 1824, by the Rev. John Webb, and published in the twentieth volume of the Archæologia. Charles Knight has also included portions of it in his "Half-Hours with the Best Authors," from which work we give the following extracts.

The author, however, it must be first premised, was a French knight, who came over to London in the spring of 1399, accompanied the unfortunate Richard in his expedition to Ireland, and remained in personal attendance upon him until he was brought prisoner to London. "I loved him sincerely," he says, "because he heartily loved the French. He gave most largely, and his gifts were profitable. Bold he was, and courageous as a lion. Right well and beautifully did he make ballads, fongs, roundels and lays. Though he was but a layman, fo gracious were all his deeds, that never I think fhall that man iffue from his country in whom God hath implanted fo much worth as was in him."

After relating, therefore, in what manner the king, then at Dublin, received the fad news of the Englifh revolt, at which he turned pale, he defcribes his hurried journey, in forrow and diftrefs, to Milford Haven. "But before he landed," fays he, "a great army which had gathered in Wales for his fervice was either difbanded or won over to Bolingbroke. In this great fear he difguifed himfelf like a poor Francifcan friar, and fet out at midnight from his hoft, attended by only a few perfons, of whom this French knight was one. He travelled hard all night, and reached Conway by break of day. There he learned that his enemies reported him to be dead, and that well nigh all was already loft."

In Shakfpeare's Richard II. we alfo find the following paffage with reference to the report of his death :—

> *Captain.*—My lord of Salifbury, we have ftaid ten days,
> And hardly kept our countrymen together,
> And yet we hear no tidings from the king;
> Therefore we will difperfe ourfelves ; farewell.
>
> *Salifbury.*—Stay yet another day, thou trufty Welfhman ;
> The king repofeth all his confidence
> In thee.
>
> *Captain.*—'Tis thought the king is dead ; we will not ftay.
> The bay trees in our country all are withered,
> And meteors fright the fixed ftars of heaven ;
> The pale-faced moon looks bloody on the earth,
> And lean-looked prophets whifper fearful change ;
> Rich men look fad, and ruffians dance and leap,
> The one in fear to lofe what they enjoy,
> The other to enjoy by rage and war :
> Thefe figns forerun the death or fall of kings.
> Farewell : our countrymen are gone and fled,
> As well affured, Richard their king is dead.

The unhappy king, on learning this report of himſelf, "uttered," ſays his chronicler, "many pious ejaculations; but he knew not what courſe to take. At length he reſolved to ſend the Duke of Exeter and the Earl of Surrey to tell Henry of Bolingbroke that he was doing much amiſs, but that he, the rightful king of England, would pardon him, and reinſtate him in all his honours and lands, if he would but defiſt. Henry, who was at Cheſter, made Exeter and Surrey his priſoners. Upon receiving this intelligence, the king, who had continued all-ſorrowful at Conway, with his intimate friends, all ſad and diſtreſſed, went ſtraight to Beaumaris. There was a ſtrong caſtle there that could not have been taken in ten years, if it had only been victualled and furniſhed with a ſufficient and faithful garriſon. But there were proviſions in none of the king's caſtles in theſe parts; and there was fidelity and affection to him in no place whatſoever. Not being able to ſtay at Beaumaris, he went to Carnarvon Caſtle, which he found totally unfurniſhed. In all his caſtles to which he retired, there was no furniture, nor had he anything to lie upon but ſtraw. Really he lay in this manner for four or ſix nights, as, in truth, not a farthing's worth of victuals or of anything elſe was to be found in them. Certes, I dare not tell the great miſery of the king."

Richard returned to Conway, he greatly bewailing his young wife, who was by this time in the hands of Bolingbroke's party. He alſo bewailed that he himſelf was in danger, both by night and day, of a cruel and certain death. While he was lying at Conway doing nothing but lamenting his hard fate, the Earl of Northumberland waited upon him from Duke Henry, who prevailed upon him to put himſelf in his hands, and truſt to the deciſion of the Engliſh Parliament; the Earl, it is ſaid, ſwearing upon the ſacrament that no harm ſhould befall him. Richard quitted Conway, and ſoon found himſelf a priſoner, for the Earl of Northumberland had placed a numerous body of troops in ambuſcade at one of the mountain-paſſes through which their journey lay. "When the king beheld them he was greatly aſtoniſhed, ſaying, 'I am betrayed! What can this be, Lord of heaven help me!' Who they were was revealed by their banners. Bitter dread prevailed; and the king demeaned himſelf ſo very ſorrowfully that it was pity to behold."

The journey of the unfortunate Richard to Flint was a very melancholy one, and of his ſufferings when there, his chronicler ſays, " no creature in this mortal world, let him be who he would, Jew or Saracen, could have beheld the king and his good friends, the Earl of Saliſbury, the Biſhop of Carliſle, Sir Stephen Scroope, and another knight named Ferriby, without being heartily ſorry for them." Nor muſt we omit one remarkable feature of this melancholy journey which would certainly make it much more hopeleſs.

"The Earl of Saliſbury told me," ſays the good French knight, " as we rode to Cheſter, that Merlin and Bede had from the time in which they lived, prophecied of the taking and ruin of the king; adding that if I were in his caſtle, he ſhould ſhow it me in form and manner as I had ſeen it come to paſs, ſaying thus—

"' There ſhall be a king in Albion, who ſhall reign for the ſpace of two and twenty years in great honour and in great power, and ſhall be allied and united with thoſe of Gaul; which king ſhall be undone in the parts of the north, in a triangular place.' Thus, the Earl told me, it was written in a book belonging to him. The triangular place he applied to the town of Conway, and for this he had a very good reaſon, for I can aſſure you it is in a triangle, as though it had been ſo laid down by a true and exact meaſurement. In the ſaid town of Conway was the king fufficiently undone; for the Earl of Northumberland drew him forth, as you have already heard, by the treaty which he made with him, and from that time he had no power. Thus the knight held this prophecy to be true, and attached thereto great faith and credit; for fuch is the nature of them in their country, that they very thoroughly believe in prophecies, phantoms, and witchcraft, and have recourfe to them right willingly. Yet," adds he, " in my opinion this is not right, but is a great want of faith."

Still more melancholy was the unhappy king's journey from Flint to Chefter.

" Thus as you heard came Duke Henry to the caftle, and fpake unto the king, to the Bifhop of Carlifle, and the two knights, Sir Stephen Scroope, and Ferriby; howbeit unto the Earl of Salifbury he fpake not at all, but fent word to him by a knight in this manner: 'Earl of Salifbury, be affured, that no more than you deigned to fpeak to my lord, the Duke of Lancafter, when he and you were in Paris at Chriftmas laft paffed, will he fpeak unto you.' Then was the Earl much abafhed, and had great fear and dread at heart, for he faw plainly that the Duke mortally hated him. The faid Duke Henry called aloud with a ftern and favage voice, ' Bring out the king's horfes;' and then they brought him out two little horfes that were not worth forty francs; the king mounted one, and the Earl of Salifbury the other. Every one got on horfeback, and we fet out from the faid caftle of Flint about two hours after mid-day. In form and manner as you have heard, did Duke Henry take king Richard, his lord, and brought him with great joy and fatisfaction to Chefter, which he had quitted in the morning. And know, that fcarcely could the thunder of heaven have been heard for the loud bruit and found of their inftruments, horns, buifines, and trumpets, infomuch that they made all the sea-shore resound with them. Thus the Duke entered the city of Chester, to whom the common people paid great reverence, praising our lord, and shouting after their king, as if in mockery."

At the time of the Welsh insurrection headed by the famous Owen Glyndwr, John de Massey was constable of Conway Castle, which it must be supposed was considered pretty strong in itself, as fifteen men-at-arms and six archers only formed its garrison, 39*s*. 2*d*. per day being allowed for the maintenance of the fortress. During the civil wars of York and Lancaster, Conway was the scene of much warfare and bloodshed, the powerful families of the Welsh in the neighbourhood taking opposite sides, and suffering accordingly. Hence Rhys, the son of Griffydd Goch, when surveying the castle from the opposite side of the river, was shot with an arrow discharged from the castle-wall by Llewellyn of Nannau, in return for which a few nights afterwards, Robin ap Griffydd Goch o'r Graianllyn, and his brother, with their followers, crossed the river, took the castle by escalade, and beheaded the captain. The whole country round was overrun by the adherents of these two factions, and utterly laid waste by the Earl of Pembroke. In 1466, Thomas ap Robin of Cochwillan was beheaded near the castle, by the Earl's orders, on account of his staunch adherence to the Lancastrian party; and his wife, it is said, carried away his head in her apron.

During the wars of the Commonwealth, Conway Castle was held as a military station of some importance, and was for some time under the command of Archbishop Williams, who was a native of the town. According to his epitaph in Llandegai Church, near Penrhyn Castle,—he being descended on his father's side from the Williams of Cochwillan, and on his mother's from the Griffiths of Penrhyn—" his great parts and eminence in all kinds of learning raifed him by the favour of King James, firft to the Deanery of Sarum, and then to that of Weftminfter." "At one and the fame time," fays the epitaph, "he was the moft intimate favourite of and privy counfellor to that great king, Lord Keeper of the Great Seal of England, and Bifhop of the fee of Lincoln, whom Charles I. honoured with the archiepifcopal mitre of York. He was thoroughly verfed in all fciences—a treafury of nine languages—the very foul of pure and undefiled theology—an oracle of political tact—the very acme and ornament of wifdom. . . . . His converfation was fweetly engaging—his memory more tenacious than human. . . . . He expended in magnificent edifices the fum of £20,000. . . . . In thofe lamentable times which followed, being worn out with the things which he faw and heard, when by fury of the rebels he could no longer ferve his king nor his country, having lived fixty-eight years, on the 25th of March, which was his birthday, with ftrong faith in Chrift and ftedfaft allegiance to the king, he moft devotedly refigned his foul to God, dying of a quinfy . . . . A.D. 1650."

The town of Conway was taken by Cromwell's army in Auguft, 1646, their victory being fignalifed by the murder of the Irifh inhabitants, who were barbaroufly tied back to back and thrown into the river. The warlike archbifhop, however, met with better treatment when, on the furrender of the caftle in the following November, he received a pardon from the parliament, and, having been wounded at Chefter, retired from military life.

At the reftoration, the caftle was granted by King Charles II. to the Earl of Conway, who as if to render it henceforth incapable of fervice either to royalift or republican, ordered it to be difmantled, and the timber, iron, and lead, of which it was deprived, were fhipped to Ireland for the repair of the

Earl's houſes in that country. The leading men of the neighbourhood, and deputy lieutenants of the county, naturally interfered to put a ſtop to this ſhameful ſpoliation, but in vain ; the following plain-ſpoken letter being his reply :—

"HONOURABLE FRIENDS,—
"I have had the honour to receive your letter of the 20th September, in which you are pleaſed to inquire of me whether my ſervant Milward doth act by my order for taking down of the lead, timber, and iron of Conway Caſtle : in anſwer to which queſtion I do by this acknowledge it to be my act and deed ; and that the ſaid Milward is employed by me to diſpoſe of the timber and iron, according to ſuch directions as I gave him, and to tranſport the lead into Ireland, where I hope it will be more ſerviceable to his ma'tie than in this country. And having this opportunity of addreſſing myſelfe to you, I humbly beſeech you to take off the reſtraint which you have put upon his proceedings, and to affoord him yor favour in it ; for I am already prejudiced by the loſſe of ſhipping and an opportune ſeaſon for the tranſportation of the lead ; yet I ſhall eſteeme this as a particular obligation vpon mee, and be ready to expreſſe it by all the ſervice in my power to every one of you, that you are pleaſed to grant this att my requeſt ; which otherwiſe may put me to ſome trouble and delay. And I doubt not of meeting occaſions to teſtifie my being,
"Honoble Sirs,
"Your affectionate and obedient Servt.
"CONWAY AND KILULTA.
"Ragley in Warwickſhire, 6th October, 1665.
"To the Honoble Thomas Bulkley, Eſq., Colonell Wynn, Hugh Wynn, Eſq., Thomas Vaughan, Eſq., his Maties Deputy-Livetenants in North Wales."

Thus was the spoliation of this beautiful edifice signed and sealed; but no advantage accrued either to the earl or to his master by this act of Vandalism, for the ships which conveyed away the materials to Ireland were wrecked on their passage—and Conway Castle from that day was left to be beautified by nature.

This romantic castle has been made the scene of various literary productions—of Monk Lewis's Castle Spectre, for instance, and Gray's Ode of the Bard, "founded," as he says, "on the tradition current in Wales, that Edward I., when he completed the conquest of that country, ordered all the bards that fell into his hands to be put to death." This bard, however, whose effusion is too Pindaric for the outpouring of a Welsh bard, took his fate into his own hands. The army of Edward, according to the poet, as they marched through a deep valley, beheld a venerable figure seated on an inaccessible rock, who with a voice more than human reproached the king with all the misery and desolation which he had brought on his country; after which, in a spirit of prophecy—the true bardic endowment—he foretold the misfortunes of the Norman race, and the future greatness and virtue of this island; after which

  Headlong from the mountain height,
  Deep in the roaring tide he plunged to endless night.

It is a fine scholastic ode, nobly conceived; but the age in which Gray wrote, rather than the poet himself, knew nothing of the true bardic mode, even if there had been the inspiration.

So much for the castle and old times: let us now take a walk into the town and see a little of the life that is going on there. It is a bright morning in August. We have been making purchases at various shops, and, having placed our several packages under the care of good Mrs. Griffiths Owen

—a ſtout, merry-faced old Welſh ſhopkeeper, who deals in bacon and butter, and ſpeaks Engliſh—we go forth on our viſit to Plas Mawr, and the other remarkable buildings of the town, the church included. Scarcely, however, have we left Mrs. Owen's, than we hear the ſound of a bell rung in the ſtreets; a bell as of a town-crier; and the next moment ſee the man himſelf proceeding along, ringing his bell loudly at intervals, but without uttering a word.

"What is the meaning of this bell being thus rung?" we inquire from a pleaſant-looking young man at a ſhop-door.

From him we learn that it is the announcement of a funeral,

CONWAY CASTLE.

which will take place in about three hours, and that this mode of invitation to the townfpeople to attend funerals is peculiar to Conway.

As this invitation might be confidered general, we determine to rank ourfelves amongft the invited, and hold ourfelves in readinefs at three o'clock for the funeral; being told, moreover, that we fhall know when to be at the church by the tolling of the church-bell.

About three o'clock accordingly,—having vifited in the meantime the fine old houfe, Plas Mawr, the ancient manfion of the Wynns, where Queen Elizabeth is faid to have ftayed, and where the initials of herfelf and her favourite, Robert Dudley, Earl of Leicefter, are frequently coupled in the carving, and feen with great fatisfaction that two of its fpacious rooms are now ufed as an infant fchool,—the church-bell began to toll, and we having added to our purchafes, fet off for the church, taking our old friend's Mrs. Griffiths Owen's on the way, to leave in her charge yet other packages. But Mrs. Owen is not in—not a foul is in. We knock on the counter again and again, and are juft about to retreat difcomfited, when a fharp-looking little lad appears from the back-fettlements, who, though he cannot fpeak Englifh, inftantly underftands our wants, and depofits our new parcels with the others under the counter. But fcarcely is this done when a voice above gabbles downftairs fomething in Welfh to the boy below, and back the boy gabbles his anfwer. Venturing on this colloquy to glance up the ftaircafe, whence the upper voice proceeds, we beheld our buxom Mrs. Owen, without her gown, a towel being about her ftout bare arms, and her face rofier than ever, from frefhly-applied foap and water. She informs us that fhe too is getting ready for the funeral; and we, being rather inquifitive regarding the dead at whofe obfequies we are intending to be prefent, fhe invites us to join her upftairs, and we follow her into her large old-fafhioned bedroom. Here, fpread out upon the large bed, lie her decent mourning bonnet, fhawl, and gown, and whilft fhe is affuming the latter, we afk if the deceafed be a relative of hers.

"No, indeed," replies fhe; "but it is right for neighbours to go to each other's funerals."

"And who, then, is going to be buried?"

Mrs. Owen's bright countenance becomes very folemn, and fhe replies :—

"A bachelor of forty; an orphan, without father or mother, and nobody left behind but a fifter, poor thing! So it is quite right to go to the funeral! And there will be many there," added fhe in an emphatic tone.

This is a convincing argument; and therefore, leaving Mrs. Owen to complete her toilet, we wend our way to the quiet old church, which ftands in the middle of the churchyard, and in the very centre of the town; gates from the various ftreets opening into the churchyard; this churchyard being, of courfe, interefting to us from Wordfworth's poem of "We are Seven."

Reaching the church, we find the large door unlocked, and enter. We are the firft of the funeral attendants; but two grey-coated tourifts, evidently father and fon, are infpecting the church; whilft a refpectable woman, in black, who is arranging and dufting the pews, anfwers any queftions which may be put to her: We too wander round, admire the fine carving on the ancient oak fcreen as we pafs into the chancel, and read the infcription on the flat grey ftone placed over the remains of "Nicholas Hookes, gentleman, who was the forty-firft child of his parents," which the younger tourift carefully copies into his note-book; and, leaving him to add that "the faid Nicholas himfelf died the father of twenty-feven children, on the 20th of March, 1637," we faunter down the ailles reading the Welſh names and titles of various noble families on the ſmall braſs plates affixed to the pew-doors, and admire the ancient carving which had been brought thither from Plas Mawr; then out at the other door to ſee if yet there be ſigns of the approaching funeral. There are none, excepting the newly-made grave cloſe by, which has juſt been dug by that young man with the ſunburnt face, who ſtands leaning on his ſpade to contemplate his work. He has ſcattered ſawduſt in the grave and piled beſide it a heap of newly-cut ruſhes. An elderly man, clad in Sunday attire, now approaches, and ſhakes hand with the young gravedigger, who at this token of ſympathy burſts into tears. What the departed was to him we know not, but with a feeling of reſpect for his grief we retire again into the church.

The grey-coated touriſts are gone, and the decent woman in black ſtands with her duſter ſtill in her hand, waiting. We remark to each other that were this fine old church near London, it would be carefully reſtored. At the name of London, the woman looks ſuddenly round, and exclaims:—

"Ah! our clock came from London; it is a bad one; more's the pity; the wind blows its fingers off! It was a preſent, and from a gentleman who did not mean it to be a bad one."

We deplore the lamentable caſe of the clock, and then inquire if ſhe ever heard of the poem, "We are Seven?"

"To be ſure I have!" ſhe anſwers. "A gentleman came once and aſked me about it; but then I had never heard of it. He ſaid, therefore, he would ſend it me from London; and ſo he did, all beautifully written out. I keep it at home; but I have ſhown it to a great many people; it is a very pretty rhyme. But for all that I've hunted the churchyard all over, and looked at every grave, but never can I find thofe of John and little Jane. I cannot make it out; certainly there muft have been fome alteration fince thofe days, for there is no cottage now by the churchyard. May-be it was pulled down years ago when a wall was built on one fide. I've often wondered how it was. But you would like to fee the verfes, wouldn't you? They are fo beautifully written out! I can run for them in a minute," added fhe eagerly. Without waiting for a reply, however, fhe fuddenly ftarted, and held up her hand liftening to the church-bell, which was ftill folemnly tolling.

"Hark!" fhe faid in an aweftricken tone, whilft a look of difmay overfpread her countenance. "Only hark how heavily the bell rings! My mother ufed to fay when it founded fo dull that it was a fure fign of another death. I have thought of it fince, and believe it to be true, though Conway is a healthy place. There is a deal of difference," fhe continued, "in the founding of the bell. My parents had the church before me; fo I know all about thefe things. I had the place after my mother."

Willing to turn her thoughts from anticipated deaths, we now inquire after the dead man, whofe funeral bell is fuch a melancholy prognoftic.

"He was Morris Evans, one of the fingers here. I knew him well," fhe replied. "When he was ftrong and came to church, his place was near the organ, amongft the fingers. Come, I will fhow it you. There," fhe faid, "this was his feat, clofe by the wall, you fee, under the carved ftone with the little figures upon it. He was ill a long time, and died of a decline, like his father and mother. There is nobody left now but his fifter and an old uncle."

At this point fome one entered to fay that the clerk was gone for the clergyman, and the funeral was moving off. We therefore took the feats which the melancholy woman affigned to us, whilft fhe ftood afide near the open door and wiped away her tears with the dufter.

The funeral is evidently on its way; a number of women and children quietly appear upon the fcene, filently filling the pews lower down the middle aifle. They are all neatly dreffed in black, many with apparently new crape on their bonnets. Here and there the bonnets or the fhawls are not black, but in fuch cafes the wearer has placed confpicuoufly fome feature of mourning about her attire. There is a great preponderance of black filks, with ftrongly-marked folds, telling of chefts and preffes out of which many have been brought from amongft other beft things. Men, too, are now in church in confiderable numbers, in dark blue cloth coats and carefully-brufhed hats, but they moftly occupy feats in the chancel and round the pulpit, having followed the bier, which half a dozen men have carried up the centre aifle, headed by the elderly clergyman in his white furplice, who as they flowly advanced, repeated by heart a pfalm in Welfh. The bearers having reverently placed the bier in the chancel, the clergyman reads from the defk part of the fifteenth chapter of the firft Epiftle to the Corinthians. To our uninitiated ears the words of the fine old language convey no confolation, but they roll on in a grand and melancholy cadence, like the notes of fome deep pathetic mufic.

The exhortation ends, and paftor and people now ftand round the open grave, whilft the burial fervice is continued in Welfh. When the benediction has been uttered, the fexton fcatters the green rufhes on the coffin; the earth is fhovelled in, and the rite is over.

The company quietly and fedately begins to difperfe; the women move off by twos and threes to other graves; little knots of men turn off in the fame way. They ftand and talk folemnly, as if of the departed whofe remains lie underneath, recalling with tender memories, perhaps, their words and deeds. Then one after another, with an undefined look of folemnity hanging about them, the townsfolk, men and women and children, move off to their refpective homes, to put afide their mourning and turn again to their different occupations.

In the meantime we ftill linger, feated upon a graveftone, and watch the laft little group which paffes out at the diftant gate. It confifts of the poor folitary fifter, overcome with grief and weeping bitterly. When buxom Mrs. Griffiths Owen fpoke of her to us, fhe had fhaken her head, faying, "fhe took it to heart, and was very low." Here then fhe was, very low and heart-broken, leaning upon the arm of a kind-looking, elderly woman, with a carefully-plaited and ftiffly-ftarched frilled cap infide her black bonnet, who feemed a very efficient prop for the bereaved mourner; after them came two other female mourners, and laftly the white-headed very old uncle, leading a fmall child by the hand. It was a mournful little group.

So ended this Welfh funeral. There was not much in it; but it impreffed us with the lovelinefs of human fympathy—the neighbourlinefs of weeping with thofe who wept.

A fcene of a different character occurred alfo juft now in Conway, which, linking to the memory and ufages of ancient times the enlarged interefts and broader views of the prefent day, brought fome hundreds of fpectators to the town, and filled the old caftle with life and gaiety.

An Eifteddfod was held here, which lafted three days, and

which, being marked by some features of national life and many picturesque details, was attractive to the tourist tribe which frequent North Wales at this season.

We are indebted to our friend the Rev. Richard Parry, of Llandudno, for most of the following information respecting Eisteddfods. He himself is a bard of the highest order, in testimony of which he is possessed of a casket of medals, gold and silver, of large size and great weight, and which, displayed upon his breast at the Conway Eisteddfod, made him a conspicuous and honoured object of attention.

The original Eisteddfod was the Parliament of the nation. The laws were founded by Dyfnwal Moelmud, four hundred years before the Christian era, and revised by Howel Dda, a thousand years ago. According to the statutes of Rhuddlan, the construction of the law was committed to the Commons, the executive to the Lords. The educational remains part and parcel of the law of the land to the present day.

An Eisteddfod was held at Conway Castle in the year 1461, in the reign of Henry VI., exactly four hundred years ago; and another during the same reign at Carmarthen, under the presidency of Gryfydd, grandfather to Sir Rhys ap Thomas, by whose aid Henry VII. was placed on the throne. On this occasion two silver badges were provided, a silver chair and a silver harp, both of which were triumphantly won by a bard and minstrel of Flintshire. Henry VIII. himself summoned an Eisteddfod at Caerwys, which was held in 1525. Queen Elizabeth did the same in 1568, the transactions of which were carefully recorded by Dr. John David Rees of Anglesey. Of later Eisteddfods, the most remarkable are one held at Denbigh in 1828, at which the Duke of Sussex presided; and one also at the same place in 1832, when her present Majesty, then Princess Victoria, distributed the prizes, and when a poem by Mrs. Hemans was read, a contribution by her to the poetical department.

After her death, an elegy to her memory being propofed as one of the fubjects of bardic compofition, the prize was won by Thomas Parry, a brother of the Rev. Richard Parry, himfelf alfo a bard of great repute, and whofe medals equal, if not exceed in number, thofe of his brother.

Befides the more ferious bufinefs of the old Eifteddfods there were triennial meetings of the Bards, at which the monarch prefided and awarded the prizes.

The compofitions produced on fuch occafions, at a time when the moft momentous events of the country were never committed to writing, affumed an important character, being the hiftorical records of the time, the expreffion of public opinion, and the affertion and maintenance of whatever great truth was agitating the beft minds of the nation. A chief bard, —the *Bardd Cadeiriog*, or chaired bard,—prefided over the order, and by virtue of his rank was placed on a feat or chair of dignity, and wore on his breaft a little filver or gold chair as a badge.

Both bards and minftrels were originally a branch of the Druidical hierarchy : the bard being the compofer of fong, the poet in fact ; the minftrel, the mufician who played on the harp, or who alfo fang with it. The pennillion finging of Wales is very ancient and remarkable ; it is improvifed finging to the equally improvifed mufic of the harper.

All knowledge, civil or religious, was anciently preferved orally, and in a metrical form for the more eafy committal to memory. The metre of their verfe was a triad or ftanza of three lines, each line compofed of feven fyllables ; the firft and fecond containing only the fubject of the poem, and the third conveying fome divine or moral precept. The bards ftill remained even after the Druids were expelled or slaughtered by the Romans; and in the sixth century, great men being amongst them, such as Aneurin Gwawdrydd, Taliesin, Llyarch Hên, and Merddyn ap Morfryn, they used their power in endeavouring to arouse their countrymen to a last great effort against the Saxons. With the conquest of Wales and the death of the last Prince Llewellyn, however, the bardic spirit was completely broken; nor did it again revive in anything like its pristine force, although it shewed signs of life in the insurrection of Owen Glyndwr. In vain the monarchs of the Tudor line, though Gray's bard beheld them as " visions of glory," endeavoured to reanimate it by royal patronage; it could not be done. In the reign of George II., however, Powell, a Welsh harper, played before the monarch, and so delighted Handel, that that great master of music composed for him several pieces, which are given in the first set of Handel's concerts. But although the old bardic spirit, in its original form, may be dead, and every effort to revive it in that form may be fruitless, because it does not belong to the character of the age, it yet exists nationally in a far wider and nobler field, throughout the Welsh people, amongst the lower orders of whom poetry is loved and cultivated, whilst their taste and feeling for music proclaims itself everywhere—in every wayside chapel and village choir.

It is judicious, therefore, in the promoters of the present Eisteddfods, to make them rather means of general enlightenment, and moral and social improvement, than attempts to revive that which is dead and belonged only to a bye-gone and semi-barbarous age. The Eisteddfod of the nineteenth century has somewhat the character of a literary institution and a social-science meeting combined. Hence, at Conway, not only were poetry and music represented, but the arts and the knowledge which embellifh and add to the comfort and advancement of domeftic and focial life. Prizes were awarded as well for treatifes on the beft management of cattle, on improvements in agricultural implements, on the beft models for veffels employed in the coafting trade, on the advantages of life-infurances, &c., on the more homely and humble female achievements of knitting and needlework, as well as for literature, poetry, and mufic.

But enough of introduction. Again we are within the walls of the old town. The morning is fine, and hundreds of people make the ftreets aftir, haftening towards the caftle to be prefent at the opening of the Eifteddfod. Flags of all colours and devices are floating from roofs and windows, and foon after leaving the railway-ftation we are aware of a band of mufic preceding a long proceffion of men, each wearing in the left-hand button-hole of his coat three golden ears of corn, with a bow of different coloured ribbon. Thefe are the committee, the bards, and the minftrels, and other fupporters of the Eifteddfod, on their way to the caftle, which they enter under a triumphal arch of laurels, flags, flowers, and various devices; a raifed pathway, formed for the occafion, leading thence into the caftle. The proceffion and mufic, however, halt in the caftle-yard, and here, with a good deal of ceremony, the Eifteddfod is proclaimed and opened with a fomewhat quaint formula of words; thus:—

"*The Truth againft the World.*—In the year one thoufand eight hundred and fixty-one, the fun approaching the autumnal equinox, in the forenoon of the fourteenth day of Auguft, after due proclamation, this Gorfedd is opened within the Royal Caftle of Conway, in Gwynedd, with invitation to all who would repair hither, where no weapon is unfheathed againft them, and judgment will be pronounced upon all works of genius fubmitted for adjudication, in the face of the fun and the eye of light."—*The Truth againft the World.*

Then with ftill further ceremony, in which a large ftone

and a large sword figure conspicuously, various candidates, women as well as men, are admitted to the enjoyment of the bardic and other honours and dignities.

As regards the stone and the sword of this ceremony, Mr. Parry says,—" In the opening proclamation it is always expressed 'where there is no naked sword against them,' or 'where there is no weapon unsheathed against them,' a symbol intended to signify that the bard is *a teacher of peace*. The presiding bard never takes the sword in hand by the hilt, but by the scabbard, half unsheathed, which the bards then graduated push up to be finally sheathed, not touching the blade. One of the questions put to the candidate for bardic orders at the *gorsedd* is, 'Wilt thou, on word and conscience, declare that thou wilt exert all thy influence to maintain peace?'

" The stone Christianity was introduced to Wales in the apostolic age; but, in fact, it was Christianity engrafted on Druidism; a mixture of both. Druidism had its essence, by tradition, from the Patriarchal religion of the land of Canaan. The stone, or the cromlech, represented Druidism: hence the ancient motto '*Da'r maen gyda'r efengyl*,' or 'The stone is good with the gospel.' "

Nor, as may be supposed, is colour without its symbolism in these ancient rites. The bard wears *blue* ribbon; the Ovate, a branch of the Druidic order representing the philosophers, physicians, mechanics, &c., *green*; and the Druids *white*.

Here also we may mention, though somewhat out of place, the pretty picturesque ancient Welsh costume worn by two young girls for the occasion, and which is always worn by a certain Mary Salsbri of Conway, who received a reward of five pounds from Lady Llanover in consequence.

In the meantime we enter the castle, the interior court of which has been transformed for the occasion into a magnificent hall, roofed in by fail-cloth fupported down the centre by mafts wreathed with evergreens. The walls, tapeftried with luxuriant ivy, are decorated with ornamental Welfh mottoes and devices, whilft a great variety of banners droop from above, confpicuous amongft which are the Prince's feathers, with the motto *Eich dyn* (your man), which the Welfh antiquarian afferts has been corrupted into ICH DIEN (I ferve).

This beautiful hall, fo appropriate for the occafion, which opened out into the old banquetting and other apartments of the caftle, was filled with feats and a raifed platform for the tranfaction of the bufinefs of the day, confpicuous on which ftood the carved chair of the chief bard, and an array of harps and other mufical inftruments. The true primitive Welfh harps, with their fimple unadorned frames of ftained wood, tall, thin, high-fhouldered inftruments, of which there were five, were naturally the moft interefting. The hall foon filled, and the leaders of the Eifteddfod, ladies as well as gentlemen, and the various muficians and fingers, took their places. The bufinefs began, and the periods of the old Welfh tongue in profe and poetry rolled grandly through the hall. But juft when the enthufiafm was growing ever warmer an unfortunate difafter occurred. It began to rain, and ere long torrents were pouring through the infecure roofing down upon the affembly. A general movement took place; mufical inftruments, and harps efpecially, were anxioufly covered by their refpective owners; umbrellas were hoifted, and people crowded together under the dry fpaces of the tent-like roof. In the meantime the bufinefs went flowly on; a fhort Welfh poem was read, but, like the rich lower notes of the finging of the Welfh nightingale, as fhe was called, was partially loft in the conftant drip, drip, of the rain, and the anxiety of everybody not to be wet through.

A difafter of this kind, however, is not without its advantages—it breaks down the barriers of filence and diftance which ftranger feels with ftranger; and, huddled under the broad green tapeftry of an ivied buttrefs, above which the rain had not yet penetrated, we ftood befide an intelligent Welfh gentleman, whofe enthufiafm no rain could damp, and from him learned various details of the gathering which otherwife we might not have known. " See, yonder intelligent-looking middle-aged Welfhwoman, in the handfome gold-coloured fhawl, and the black ftraw hat worn above the lace, pink-trimmed cap,—fhe is a Welfh bardefs from South Wales, who has carried off already feveral prizes at former Eifteddfods, and is here perhaps for new honours." And what a fingularly acute countenance hers was, with the clear brown eyes and well-cut Roman nofe! " And yonder young peafant man, with the fenfitive and almoft refined features, and the thin yellow beard,—he alfo is a bard, Llewelyn Twrog by name—who has juft read a very clever poem addreffed to the Eifteddfod by another bard, quite a patriarch, Abfolom Vardd, upwards of eighty years of age."

We turn now to the platform. The great harp conteft was that morning to have taken place, and as more than the ufual prizes had been offered for the occafion, the excitement and expectation were proportionately great. The time was almoft at hand, but the pitilefs rain came down fafter than ever. " Look now at yonder pale, thin boy," faid our friend ; " he is not fo tall as his harp, but he is a marvellous performer, and probably will carry off the chief prize." We had already noticed him, and efpecially becaufe fome defect of fight, apparently almoft blindnefs, had awakened our fympathy. It was a grave, melancholy face, though fo young, with little of a boy's joyoufnefs, and nothing of his reckleffnefs about it ; the young foul of which it was the outward index dwelt in an inner world brighter than this—a world of harmony and higher vifion. A fimple peafant-woman, his mother as we fuppofed, was with him; but this, as we learned afterwards, was not the cafe; neverthelefs, fhe was his friend, and helped him when the rain began, to cover his harp, as the other harpers had done theirs, that the ftrings might be kept dry. But now that the harp conteft is expected to take place, every harper is bufy with his inftrument, and you hear a tuning of ftrings in preparation. Behind the boy is a fomewhat grand, peafant-like man, whofe breaft is covered with medals, and he too is almoft blind. He is a celebrated harper from South Wales, the fuccefsful candidate in many former contefts, and now, he or the boy, our friend tells us, will in all probability carry away the increafed prize. The woman lifts the covering from the boy's harp, whilft his thin, fmall, nervous fingers try the ftrings, firft one and then another. Very jealoufly the woman lifts it, juft far enough to admit the little hand and no farther.

But the rain forbade this moft interefting conteft, which indeed only took place on the laft day, when, as our friend had predicted, the many-medalled harper and the boy were the victors. They, however, in the firft place, contefted fo equally, that a fecond trial was called for, when the boy carried off the firft, and the man the fecond prize.

One feature of thefe national gatherings fhould not be overlooked, namely, the enlarged knowledge of the language to which they lead. Half a century ago, when the Welfh tongue was fpoken even more univerfally than now, it was difregarded by the higher and educated claffes, and there was fcarcely a fingle Welfh clergyman of the Church of England in a Welfh pulpit—hence one caufe of the immenfe growth of diffent in Wales, and of the number of little chapels which you find everywhere. Now however, on the contrary, when the Englifh mingle more than ever with the Welfh, and the Englifh language is taught in their eftablifhed village fchools, every church,

R

however infignificant, has its univerfity-educated native clergyman, who preaches in eloquent Welfh, and many of whom, as well as the native nobility and gentry, pay great attention to the language as a rich philological ftudy, and difcover in it traces of the higheft antiquity, clofe kinfhip even to the oldeft and nobleft languages of the earth. In this refpect alfo the Eifteddfod may be called a national college. Neverthelefs, it is to be wifhed that whilft all means fhould be ufed to preferve this fine old language as a fpoken tongue, Englifh were more generally underftood by the people; pious, intelligent people as they are; but whofe *dim Saffenach* makes them as fealed books to the friendly Englifh tourift or refident. But ftill, the power, deep fentiment, and mufical cadence of this remarkable language, are often exhibited even to thefe in the little prayer meetings of the wayfide or village chapel, where the impaffioned and eloquent utterances of the foul are poured forth in the minor key, with an eloquence and pathos which even a Beethoven could not furpafs.

Before clofing this long article on Conway, we muft mention with approbation the good tafte and judgment with which the great works of modern improvement and civilization—the fufpenfion bridge, and the railway-works—are made, not only to harmonize with the caftle, but even to add to it new features of beauty and dignity.

The caftle is the property of the Crown, but is now held by Lady Erfkine.

Goodrich Castle and Court.

Through shattered galleries, 'mid roofless halls,
Wandering with timid footstep oft betrayed,
The stranger sighs, nor scruples to upbraid
Old Time; though He, gentlest among the thralls
Of Destiny, upon these wounds hath laid
His lenient touches, soft as light that falls
From the wan moon, upon the towers and walls,
Light deepening the profoundest sleep of shade.
Relic of kings! wreck of forgotten wars,
To winds abandoned, and the prying stars,
Time *loves* thee! At his call the seasons twine
Luxuriant wreaths around thy forehead hoar;
And, though past pomp no changes can restore,
A soothing recompense, his gifts, are thine!

WORDSWORTH.

NE of the most striking beauties of the river Wye, is the tendency which it has to strike out fine circles in its course, sometimes almost as true as if struck by compasses. These, amid alternating rocks and woods, and verdant meadows, are not only delightful to the eye themselves, but give to the advancing traveller all the charms of rural beauty. One of these fine sweeps occurs at Goodrich, about four miles from Rofs, in Herefordshire, and on a bold promontory encircled thus by the beautiful stream, stand the remains of Goodrich Castle, till the time of the wars of the Commonwealth one of the strongest fortresses of England.

This caftle was granted in the fifth year of King John to William Marfhall, Earl of Pembroke, who married Ifabel, the fole heirefs of the famous Strongbow, conqueror of Ireland, and fucceeded to his vaft eftates. He was the fame Earl of Pembroke who advifed Henry III. to grant the Great Charter. It afterwards went into the family of the De Valences, from whom it paffed by marriage to the Talbots, Earls of Shrewsbury, and remained theirs till 1616, when Gilbert, the feventh Earl, left three daughters his coheireffes. To one of thefe, Elizabeth, fell Goodrich, and fhe carried it by marriage to her hufband, Henry Grey, Earl of Kent, who died in 1639 without iffue. The caftle and eftate then paffed to his next relatives, who became Earls and afterwards Dukes of Kent. At the demife of Henry, the laft Duke of Kent of that family, it paffed by purchafe in 1740 to the Griffins of Hadnock: and a few years ago it was bought by Sir Samuel Rufh Meyrick, of Goodrich Court.

The caftle is moft famous for the ftout refiftance that it made in 1646, when it was held for the king by Sir Richard Lingen, againft the Parliament force under Colonel Birch, to whom, however, it was eventually compelled to furrender.

It appears that Colonel Birch marched out of Hereford on the morning of March the 10th, with a party of horfe and foot, and was joined at Goodrich by the horfe of Colonel Kirle from Monmouth, and the firelocks of Rumfey. They fell on the ftables and took fixty-four horfes, with hay and other provifions. They burnt down the ftables, and then went into the paffage-houfe, feized the officers and foldiers in it, and invefted the caftle. The fiege continued till the 31ft of July, nearly four months. The caftle was exceedingly ftrong, being built on a rock, and of the ftone dug out of the ditch, fo that the ditch was very deep, and the walls and towers were raifed on maffive pyramidal baftions, like fome of the towers at Chepftow. The nearer approach to the caftle was defended by a fucceffion of gates and deep foffes and drawbridges. What thefe defences were may be imagined from this recent defcription :—" The body of the keep is an exact fquare of twenty feet. The additions made to

GOODRICH CASTLE.

this fortrefs down to the time of Henry VI. begin with the very ftrongly fortified entrance, which, commencing between two femicircular towers of unequal dimenfions, near the eaft angle, was continued under a dark vaulted paffage to an extent of fifty feet. Immediately before this entrance, and within the space enclosed by the fosse, was a very deep pit, hewn out of the solid rock, formerly crossed by a drawbridge, which is now gone. About eleven feet within this passage was a massy gate. This gate and the drawbridge were defended on each side by loopholes, and overhead by rows of machicolations for pouring down melted lead, etc., on the heads of assailants. Six feet and a half beyond this was a portcullis, and about seven further a second portcullis; and the space between these was again protected by loopholes and machicolations. About two feet more inward was another strong gate, and five feet and a half beyond this on the right a small door leading to a long, narrow gallery, only three feet high, formed in the thickness of the wall, and which was the means of access to the loopholes in the eastern tower, as well as to some others that commanded the brow of the steep precipice towards the North-east. These works appear to have been thought sufficient for general defence; but a resource was ingeniously contrived for greater security in case they had been forced, for a little further on are massy stone projections in the wall on each side, like pilasters, manifestly designed for inserting great beams of timber within them, like bars from one side of the passage to the other, so as to form a strong barricade, with earth or stones between the rows of timber, which would in a short time form a strong, massy wall."

In the days of mere bows and battle-axes this would have been found an unassailable stronghold, and even Colonel Birch, with such cannon and mortars as they had in those days, seems to have been rather staggered by the sturdy strength of the place; for when he had lain before it till the beginning of June, he wrote to the Committee of Parliament begging for battering cannon; "or else," he said, "I may sit long enough before it." He had, up to that time, it appears, only two mortar-pieces, but the great iron culverin was going from Gloucefter, and two guns from Ludlow. He reported the enemy very refolute within, and very careful of their ammunition, trufting to their ftrong walls. On the 1ft of June he began to make regular approaches " within piftol-fhot of the enormous rampiers, intending when they were finifhed to fhoot granadoes in the mortar-pieces." The prifoners they had taken informed them that the befieged were well fupplied with provifions, and depended much on the ftrength of the caftle. On the 13th of June, Birch fummoned them to furrender, offering them flattering terms, but they only laughed at them. Whereupon they began to ftorm with their granadoes, and tore down a piece of a tower. Still the befieged only laughed at them; and when they faw fappers at work preparing mines at the bafe of the caftle, one of the Cavaliers called out, faying, " they cared not for being blown up, they could from the fky laugh at the flourifhing Roundheads." On the 15th of June Colonel Birch complained that his ordnance was fmall, and had done but little execution. He had, therefore, fent for two great guns : all that had yet been done having been performed by the two mortar-pieces. But he reported that the mines were going on well. Another letter on the 18th of July, reported that they had made a breach in an upper wall, and that the granadoes had done much damage, but " yet they take no more notice of it than if no enemy were before it." Yet the writer flatters himfelf that the great mortar-piece and the mine would make them foon cry for mercy," and he trufts that the eftate of Sir Richard Lingen would make amends both to the ftate and the befiegers. We muft fuppofe that the great mortar-piece and the mine had all the effect that the writer anticipated, for on the 31ft of July the befieged had furrendered on promife of their lives. This was the laft caftle which held out for the king, except that of Pendennis. The caſtle was difmantled by order of Parliament.

On the North ſide, where are windows for reconnoitering the Wye, there is a charming profpect over the adjacent country. On the Weſt are the remains of the banquetting-hall: and on the Eaſt thoſe of the chapel, with an ornamented Gothic window. Near the hall is a curious octagonal column, evidently the centre round which the grand ſtaircaſe was carried, but that and the tower encloſing it are deſtroyed.

In the Memoirs of Wordſworth, we learn that the little girl who is the heroine of his poem, "WE ARE SEVEN," the poet met with, not at Conway, where by poetic licenſe he has laid the ſcene, but within the area of Goodrich Caſtle, in the ſpring of 1793: and thus the myſtery is ſolved of the little girl ſpeaking Engliſh, or the poet ſo fully underſtanding Welſh. Hence in vain, though " the grave is green, it may be ſeen," has the good woman of Conway, and no doubt many another perſon, hunted for it in Conway churchyard.

> A ſimple child,
> That lightly draws its breath,
> And feels its life in every limb,
> What ſhould it know of death?
>
> I met a little cottage girl,
> She was eight years old, ſhe ſaid;
> Her hair was thick with many a curl
> That cluſtered round her head.
>
> She had a ruſtic, woodland air,
> And ſhe was wildly clad:
> Her eyes were fair, and very fair;
> — Her beauty made me glad.
>
> "Siſters and brothers, little maid,
> How many may you be?"
> "How many? Seven in all," ſhe ſaid,
> And wondering looked at me.

"And where are they? I pray you tell."
  She anfwered, "Seven are we;
And two of us at Conway dwell,
  And two are gone to fea.

"Two of us in the churchyard lie,
  My fifter and my brother;
And, in the churchyard cottage, I
  Dwell near them with my mother."

"You fay that two at Conway dwell,
  And two are gone to fea;
Yet ye are feven!—I pray you tell,
  Sweet maid, how this may be."

Then did the little maid reply,
  "Seven boys and girls are we;
Two of us in the churchyard lie,
  Beneath the churchyard tree."

"You run about, my little maid,
  Your limbs they are alive;
If two are in the churchyard laid,
  Then ye are only five."

"Their graves are green, they may be feen,"
  The little maid replied;
"Twelve fteps or more from my mother's door,
  And they are fide by fide.

"My ftockings there I often knit,
  My kerchief there I hem;
And there upon the ground I fit -
  I fit and fing to them.

"And often after funfet, Sir,
  When it is light and fair;
I take my little porringer,
  And eat my fupper there.

"The firft that died was little Jane;
  In bed fhe moaning lay;
Till GOD releafed her of her pain,
  And then fhe went away.

"So in the churchyard fhe was laid,
  And when the grafs was dry,
Together round her grave we played,
  My brother John, and I.

"And when the ground was white with fnow,
  And I could run and flide;
My brother John was forced to go,
  And he lies by her fide."

"How many are you then," faid I,
  "If they two are in Heaven?"
The little maiden did reply,
  "O Mafter! we are feven."

"But they are dead; thofe two are dead!
  Their fpirits are in Heaven!"
'Twas throwing words away: for ftill
The little maid would have her will,
  And faid, "Nay, we are feven!"

In the memoirs of Wordfworth we alfo find this entry:—
"In the fpring of 1841 I revifited Goodrich Caftle; the river from its pofition and features is a moft impreffive object. I could not but deeply regret that its folemnity was impaired by a fantaftic new caftle (Goodrich Court), fet up on a projection of the fame ridge, as if to fhow how far modern art can go in furpaffing all that could be done by antiquity and nature, with their united graces, remembrances, and affociations."

We may imagine with what aftonifhment our late friend, Sir Samuel Meyrick, would have read this paragraph had it been publifhed in his life-time. Sir Samuel, fo far from endeavouring to caft into the fhade ancient art by modern, was the zealous admirer of all antiquity. This building was defigned and executed as an expofition of the principles of feudal architecture, and intended to contain thofe collections of ancient armour and other feudalities which he had accumulated at fo much expenfe. It was projected to exemplify the ftyle of architecture prevailing during the reigns of Edwards I., II., and III. It was defigned by Blore, and the firft ftone was laid on the 23rd of April, 1828, by Llewellyn Meyrick, Sir Samuel's only fon, who was not deftined to live to inherit this charming place. Sir Samuel himfelf died in 1848, and the property paffed to his nephew, Colonel Meyrick, of the Scots Fufilier Guards. Goodrich Court ftands firmly on a bold promontory of the Wye, with a wood running down the fteep bank to the river. It is backed by Coppet Wood and hills at fome diftance, giving it a pofition of peculiar beauty. Sir Samuel Meyrick, the author of the fplendid work on " Ancient Armour," had filled this manfion with a collection of objects, which, if they had not won over the poetic mind of Wordsworth from cenfure to praife, would have enchanted the feudal taftes of Sir Walter Scott.

Goodrich Court is approached from the highway from Rofs to Monmouth by an arched gateway, called the Monmouth Gateway, at about the diftance of half a mile from the houfe itfelf. Arriving, you pafs over the moat by a drawbridge leading to a gateway, furnifhed duly with its portcullis, and flanked by two round towers. You then find yourfelves on a fine airy terrace overlooking the Wye far below, and in front of the building, prefenting a variety of round towers, gables, and turrets, full of detail, but fomewhat wanting in elevation to confer on it the full dignity of a feudal fortrefs. In fact, with all its intended ftyle of antiquity, there is a modern afpect about it, not merely refulting from its frefhnefs, but from the mixture of gothic façades, more appropriate to a monaftery than a caftle. The chief tower is flanked with a ftrong baftion, is machicolated, and furnifhed with lantern, turrets and fpire.

The building inclofes a fpacious court, which is divided

into two by the grand armoury. A porch on the left side of the inner court leads you to the entrance-hall. In a cavetto moulding over the archway in characters of the time of Edward II., is the following inscription : —
AUSPICE EDV. BLORE.
SUMPTIBUS S. R. MEYRICK.
A.D. MDCCCXXVIII.
In the spandrels of the arch, on each side, is a stone shield, sculptured with armorial bearings of the family. On the door is a bronze knocker, designed by Giovanni di Bologna, representing the destruction of the Philistines by Samson. The entrance-hall is divided by an archway, and is adorned with arms, hunting weapons, stags'-horns, etc., displayed with great taste. The fire-place, of Painswick stone, is finely designed by Mr. Blore, the architect; but the great curiosity of the hall is a Bohemian pavoise, of the middle of the fifteenth century. The hall at night is lighted by a Greek lamp found in Herculaneum, rich in ornaments of female masks and horses' heads; a head of Janus forming the lid of the receptacle for the oil. On the principal door is a curious carving of George and the Dragon, of the time of Henry VII., in which the dragon holds his meat-dish in his paws, containing the king's daughter ready to be devoured. In the part leading to the staircase is a fine oriel window, richly emblazoned with painted glass, representing Sir Samuel's ancestor, Meuric or Meyrick ab Llewellyn, of Bodorgan, in the island of Anglesey, esquire of the body to King Henry VII., with the family arms, crest and motto. From the hall a sallyport with drawbridge leads to the Ladies' Terrace; thence by another drawbridge you cross the moat to the flower-garden, and thence you can descend through the wood to the river.

To the left of the entrance-hall you pass into the gallery of

Henry VI., the length of which is one hundred and fix feet. The window is an admirable fpecimen of German painted glafs, reprefenting St. George in fluted armour, with the date 1517. On the right hand, in a niche, ftands a figure accoutred in probably the moſt magnificent fuit of armour in exiſtence: beautifully emboffed with bas-reliefs, and inlaid with gold. It belonged to the Duke of Ferrara, the patron of Taffo. It is one of thofe gleanings of the world with which Buonaparte intended to enrich Paris, and was defigned for Malmaifon, but did not reach France before Buonaparte was dethroned in 1814, and was purchafed at Modena by Sir Samuel.

Quitting the entrance-hall on the right, you are introduced to the ASIATIC GALLERY, in which are arranged a great number of articles of coftume, arms, armour, etc., from India, China, and other parts of Afia. The room is papered to imitate the walls of the Alhambra in Spain, and there is a figure in Moorifh armour brought from Spain, made of pieces of hide cut into fcales, and refembling the lorica of the Romans. In the centre is a Pindaree warrior on horfeback. The chain-armour of the warrior and the trappings of the horfe were brought by Captain Grindley from India, the headgear being of folid filver. The whole group was prepared from a drawing by Captain Grindley. There are two glafs cafes filled with arms and armour from various countries of Afia, including China. Behind this, feparated from the anteroom by a row of arches, is the ASIATIC ARMOURY, in which is a grand group of Indian figures on horfeback, to exhibit varieties of Indian and Perfian armour and coftume. There is another glafs-cafe containing arms and other articles; and two others, one on each fide of the window, containing a variety of Hindoo deities and Chinefe curiofities. Then comes the SOUTH SEA ROOM, fimilarly furnifhed with the weapons from the iflands of the Pacific, including a grand war-cloak of feathers, brought from the Sandwich Ifles by Captain Cook. Thefe rooms are curious and inftructive, but they are the leaft of all like what you are looking for in a Britifh baronial hall: you enter with a more fatisfied feeling the oppofite fuite of rooms.

The BANQUETTING HALL ftrikes you as perfect. It is fifty feet long. Over the entrance is the Minftrels' Gallery, and on the dais or raifed floor at the upper end is a billiard table, on one fide of which folding doors conduct to a covered way leading to the ftables; on the other fide other folding-doors lead to the HASTILUDE CHAMBER. The roof is of oak, high pitched, refting on ftone corbels; the floor and panelling are alfo of oak, and the chimney-piece is elaborately carved in Painfwick ftone, bearing on its pediment an alto-relievo of Aylmer de Valence, the owner of the caftle in the time of Edward II., copied from his monument in Weftminfter Abbey. From this window there are fine views of Goodrich Caftle, and of the valleys of the Wye and of Lea Bailey. Amongft the paintings in this room are Phillip II. of Spain, by Coello, the Spanifh Court painter; his daughter Ifabella and her hufband Ferdinand; Lord Howard of Effingham; the Queen of James II., and Henry, Prince of Wales; Villiers, Duke of Buckingham, in armour, by Cornelius de Neve; a trooper of the Commonwealth, faid to be Cornet Joyce, and portraits of Sir Samuel and his fon.

In the HASTILUDE CHAMBER you find yourfelves in the midft of a tournament,—men, fteeds, fpectators, lifts, heralds, the royal box, and the whole coftume and appurtenances of the fame. You have alfo, in the fame room, if our memory ferve us right, the proceffion of Sir Samuel himfelf when high fheriff, with all his javelin-men in his livery. Near this is a

CHAPEL, fitted as all chapels were at the fuppofed date, the time of our Edwards, in the Roman Catholic ftyle. The carvings and figures are many of them of thofe times, others of Henry VI. The rich altar-cloth, the large candlefticks, the croziers, the reading defks, and other fittings, are all ancient and curious from their hiftories. But the efpecial room of the houfe is THE GRAND ARMOURY. It is eighty feet in length, and you have the hiftory of ancient armour before your eyes on the backs of figures reprefenting known warriors, ten of thefe figures on horfeback. You have alfo ten glafs-cafes, containing a feries of arms and armour, down from the Greek and Roman and the Ancient Briton, to the time when armour was exploded by that terrible explofive, gunpowder. Above thefe are ranged banners of many famous men; and in the intervening fpaces are eighty-four halberds, arranged in groups according to their refpective periods. The oaken columns fupporting the gallery are covered with weapons of all known kinds, including the moft complete collection of the kind in the world. It was the poffeffion of this unrivalled affemblage of arms and armour which enabled Sir Samuel to write and illuftrate his fuperb work on the fubject. We believe that it was from this armoury that the Auftrians adopted the fame arrangement in the great armoury in one of the palaces in Vienna.

It is an odd feeling that haunts you when walking amongft this extenfive collection of inftruments of death. You feem to have ftepped out of the Chriftian world altogether, and entered one of animals, bent above all things on mutual deftruction. What a wonderful exertion of the faculties, from age to age, to devife fome newer and more efficient means of fending people out of the world! What an inveterate race of fteel porcupines in the fhape of men! If any one ever doubted of the fall, and that "the heart of man is deceitful above all things, and defperately wicked," it would not, it feems to us, be poffible to doubt it for half-an-hour in fuch a gallery as this. The ingenious inventions, and the coftly productions, of many races and generations of people priding themfelves at once on being Chriftians and exterminators of Chriftians: fons of the Prince of Peace inveterately given to fighting. Such a difplay of the weapons of death feems, indeed, to fubftantiate the doctrine of the late actuary Finlayfon, that "war is the *natural* condition of man, and peace is but the feafon of exhauftion, and of recruiting himfelf for frefh encounters of reciprocal murders. What a fingular idea this gives us of the human race!—what a difmal illuftration of univerfal hiftory! That unhappy thing so happily called—'the great river of mingled blood and tears.'"

Goodrich Court is for the moft part thrown open to public infpection, and is reforted to by throngs of deeply interefted vifitors: but it is only by thofe who, like ourfelves, have fpent fome time in the houfe, that the vaft extent of its treafures of art and antiquity can be known. There is a fuite of apartments referved for the family, and not opened to the public. There are the library, the dining, breakfaft, and drawing rooms, the Doucean Mufeum, the Sir Gelly Chamber, the chambers fitted up in the fafhion of and named after James I.; Charles I. and Charles II.'s Galleries; William III.'s Chamber, with the Prince's, the Herald's, the Page's, and the Leech's chambers, and the Greek Room. In thefe rooms are contained a wealth of articles of ancient art and vertu, of paintings and fculptures and gems, that fill a large catalogue. We may, however, mention one or two particulars. Mifs Strickland in the "Hiftory of the Queens of England," wonders what has become of a certain ivory box, carved in the fhape of a rofe, mentioned by Horace Walpole to have contained the miniature portraits of Henry VIII. and Anne of Cleves, painted by Holbein, and which, by the over-flattering likenefs of Anne, occafioned fo much mifchief. This is fecurely depofited in a drawer of the library, and we muft fay that if Anne had been as comely-looking as there reprefented, even Henry could not have complained of her plainnefs. The library table is of the time of Henry III., and amongft the valuable collection of books is the original edition of 1521, of Henry VIII.'s *Affertio Septem Sacramenta, contra M. Luther*, which obtained for Henry the title of Defender of the Faith, from the Pope; with a curious frontifpiece by Hans Holbein. There are alfo other relics of Henry VIII., and portraits of Luther and his wife, Catherine à Boria. On the table of the drawing-room is a pair of enamelled copper candlefticks, feven hundred years old, with an inkftand and other articles of nearly the fame age. The Doucean Mufeum contains the rich collection of works of art and antiquity, collected by Mr. Francis Douce, and bequeathed by him to Sir Samuel Meyrick, confifting of paintings of the Byzantine and Italian fchools, tapeftry, drawings, engravings, carvings in wood and ivory, enamels, cinquecent bronzes, coins and medals, crefts, antiquities of Greece, Egypt, Rome, Mexico, Perfia, China, and India. Befides this every room has its appropriate fittings and objects of hiftoric and artiftic intereft. During our vifit at Goodrich Court we were lodged in the chamber of William and Mary.

Fountains Abbey.

NO part of England in the palmy days of Romanism could boast more splendid monastic buildings, or can now show more magnificent remains of them, than Yorkshire. Greatly varied in its scenery, this extensive county is traversed by dales and glens, presenting every attraction to that love of seclusion, and yet of stately half religious, half baronial life, which distinguished the sacred orders of the Roman church. Woods and rivers, and fair uplands, and wild forest tracks, gave every scope for the love of solitude, of the pomp and harmony of worship, or for the more worldly tastes for the chace, and the tributes of fish and *feræ naturæ*, and bovine and pecudine substantials for the refectory. Fountains and Rievaux, Jervaux and Byland, and many another name, raise visions of the now shattered grandeur of the monastic ages, that had nothing to outvie it in any country of Europe. Of all these, and of all such superb seats of conventual power and splendour in England, none can equal in extent of ruin, as once in amplitude of estate, the noble pile of Fountains. We are told that after its original period of poverty and distress, a great prosperity flowed in upon the establishment. Many persons of power and opulence purchased, by large donations, a sepulture within the walls of the abbey. Favoured by popes, kings, and pre-

FOUNTAINS ABBEY; FROM THE ABBOT'S HOUSE.

lates, with various immunities and privileges, and enriched by a fucceffion of princely gifts, Fountains Abbey became one of the wealthieft monafteries of the kingdom. The church ranked amongft the faireft ftructures of the land, and the poffeffions attached to it comprehended a vaft extent, embracing the country from the foot of Pennigent to the boundaries of St. Wilfrid of Ripon, an uninterrupted fpace of more than thirty miles. Befides many other wide domains, the lands in Craven contained, in a ring fence, a hundred fquare miles, or fixty thoufand acres, on a moderate computation.

We learn from the "Monafticon," on the authority of

Hugh, a monk of Kirkſtall, that the ſite of this monaſtery was granted in 1132, by Thurſton, Archbiſhop of York, out of his liberty of Ripon, which town, containing the venerable cathedral of St. Wilfrid, is not four miles off. He conferred it on certain monks, who ſeparated themſelves from what they deemed the lax diſcipline of the Benedictine abbey of St. Mary of York, and reſolved to adopt the Ciſtercian rule, which was then becoming famous from the reputed ſanctity and daring enthuſiaſm of St. Bernard. Richard, the prior, with the ſub-prior, ten monks of St. Mary's, and Robert, a monk of Whitby, retired in the depth of winter to this ſecluded, and, at that period, wild and uncultivated dell, where they commenced a church in honour of the Bleſſed Virgin. They found ſhelter, according to tradition, under a gigantic elm, which is ſaid to have lived on for four hundred years; and, if ſo, probably only fell with the abbey itſelf, for the royal commiſſioners of Henry VIII. arrived to pronounce its doom in 1535. There are alſo remaining old yews ſtill ſtanding near the abbey mill, and probably planted by the firſt fathers of the place. Like the founders of many other monaſteries, the monks were at firſt nearly driven away by ſtarvation. They determined to accept the invitation of St. Bernard to go over and take refuge in his monaſtery of Clairvaux, in Champagne, but juſt at this juncture good fortune began to ſmile on them; they remained, and the monaſtery grew into the ſplendour and the wealth which we have mentioned.

The hiſtory of Fountains Abbey is like hundreds of other ſuch houſes. In ſome contentions in its earlier days between Murdoc, its abbot, and one William, for election to the archbiſhopric of York, the partizans of William ſet fire to it, and burnt it down, hoping to have burnt Murdoc in it. It was ſoon rebuilt, for the ſtyle of the main body of the abbey is

Early English, and though many additions were made to it, they muſt have been either very early, or only towards the conclufion of the papal afcendancy in England ; for the main body of the building is in the Early Englifh ſtyle, and the tower in the Perpendicular. We are told that in 1203, Ralph, the ninth abbot, commenced the building of the choir, and that fucceſſive abbots built the Lady Chapel, or chapel of the Nine Altars, and that theſe, with the great cloiſter, the Infirmary, and the Xenodochium, or houſe of entertainment for the poor, were not completed till 1247. The great tower appears to have been built by the abbots Huby and Darnton at the end of the fifteenth century, and is of the ſtyle of that period, the Perpendicular ; ſo that it muſt have been in the glory of its freſhneſs when the commiſſioners of Henry VIII. arrived in 1535 to terminate its eccleſiaſtical exiſtence. It was finally ſurrendered in 1539 by Marmaduke Bradley, thirty-eighth abbot. According to the certificates delivered to the commiſſioners, its income, including the tythes, was £998 6s. 7½d., but it appears by another account to have realized annually £1,173 0s. 7d.

The abbey and part of the eſtates were ſold by Henry VIII. to Sir Richard Greſham, the father of Sir Thomas Greſham, the founder of the Royal Exchange in London. In the eighteenth century, the property was purchaſed by William Aiſlabie, the ſon of Mr. Chancellor Aiſlabie, the proprietor of the adjoining property of Studley Royal, alſo an original domain of the Abbey of Fountains, which had paſſed through the hands of the families of Aleman, Le Gros, Tempeſt, and Mallory ; John Aiſlabie, the Chancellor of the Exchequer at the beginning of the eighteenth century, having inherited it from Mary Mallory, his mother. The two properties were thrown together by the ſon of the Chancellor, the purchaſer of Fountains, and now conſtitute a property having few rivals for picturefque beauty. From William Aiflabie it defcended to the late Mrs. Lawrence, famous for her political fpirit, and for triumphing over the very Reform Bill, and continuing, by the creation of what were called cowfhed votes, to fend her nominees for the adjoining borough of Ripon to parliament. By her it was bequeathed to the Earl de Grey, a collateral defcendant from the Aiflabies, who is now the fortunate proprietor.

To reach the abbey, you muft prefent yourfelf at the gates of Studley Park, where guides are in attendance to conduct you over the whole fcene. With one of thefe you afcend the vale of the Skell, amid a fucceffion of fcenes of the moft woodland and truly Englifh beauty. As you advance, you behold unfolding before you, woods, grand old avenues, lakes, ftreams, fountains, and lawns and terraces of the moft fmoothly-fhaven neatnefs. It is the perfection of art employed on a wildly fecluded nature. The exquifite keeping and finifh of the whole makes you feel as if you had entered the very gardens of Armida, if even they in their fabled beauty can be conceived fo highly adorned and exquifitely tended.

> In fhadier bowers,
> More facred and fequeftered, though but feigned,
> Pan or Sylvanus never flept, nor nymph
> Nor faunus haunted.
> MILTON.

In fact, the artiftic finifh appears almoft too perfect, and as if not a leaf even could fall without offending that confummate polifh of velvet lawn, winding walk, fmooth as polifhed ftone, and bower, and temple, grotto, and ftatue of Grecian god or goddefs, or contending gladiators, the hum of nicely-ftudied waterfall, or the funlit furface of lakes, moved only by the wings and oaring feet of wild fowl. But, as thefe elyfian scenes are but the introduction to the abbey itself, we shall only say that we pass the Moon and Crescent ponds, the Octagon Tower, leaving Studley Hall itself on the right, and through groups of immense spruce firs, some of them of one hundred and thirty feet in height, and of upwards of twelve feet in circumference at the base. Suddenly a door opens, and we find ourselves in a noble Gothic alcove, called Anne Boleyn's Seat, and before us a most striking view of the abbey, with its tall and stately tower, amid the opening woods, and on the banks of the meandering Skell.

As we advance along this narrow dale amid towering rocks and shrouding woods, we are reminded that we are now in Fountain Dale, famous for the contest of Robin Hood and the Curtal friar. Passing this spot, we presently emerge into the full view of the noble abbey, with the fine pointed windows of the body of the church wreathed with masses of ivy; but its grand tower standing clear and majestic, and nearly as unimpaired as at the hour of its desertion. To describe the whole of the remains of this admirable ruin would require a volume. There are the chapel of Nine Altars, the glorious choir, the transept and side chapels, the tower, the nave, the cloister-court, the cloisters, and chapter-house—all demanding particular attention for their noble proportions, and the grace and beauty of their remaining arches, columns, and windows. The chapel of Nine Altars is wonderfully impressive from the loftiness and lightness of its arches, which cross it in prolongation of the clerestory of the choir, the central pillars of which are octagonal, but are now stripped of the cylindric shafts, with which they were formerly clustered. These are said to have been the work of a rustic genius of the village of Sawley, called in the charters of the abbey "Thomas Marmorarius de Sawley." Over one of the windows is a scroll inscribed in abbreviation

with a motto which reveals the origin of the abbey's name.—
𝔅𝔢𝔫𝔢𝔡𝔦𝔠𝔦𝔱𝔢 𝔣𝔬𝔫𝔱𝔢𝔰 𝔡𝔬𝔪𝔦𝔫𝔬.

In the choir only the external walls remain; but on the two upper greces of the High Altar have been relaid a portion of that "painted floor" recorded to have been beftowed on the choir by the abbot, John de Cantia, in the thirteenth century, confifting of tefleræ of red, black, yellow, and grey. There is alfo a ftone coffin, faid to be that of Lord Percy of Alnwick, who was buried before the high altar in 1315; and a huge black marble graveftone of the abbot, John de Ripon. In the fide chapels of the tranfept are other remains, particularly of the tomb of Abbot Burley: and on each fide of the great tower, above and below the belfry windows, are infcriptions in Tudor black letter boldly relieved. The infcriptions above the windows are all different, but the fame individual motto ferves for the lower infcription on all four fides.—" Soli deo honor et gloria in fecula feculorum. Amen." The Cloifter Court remains furrounded by the church and its accompanying buildings. It is one hundred and twenty-five feet fquare. On the weft of it are the cloifters themfelves, ftill perfect, and prefenting a double arcade of arches. It is lighted by windows looking into the court, but prefents a folemn and fombre twilight fcene; and when the imagination raifes the figures of the ancient monks, in cowls and frocks, taking their exercife here in winter, the impreffions of their life and times come vividly before us. So narrow is the valley here that a great part of thefe cloifters are built over the river, the floor being laid on arches. Over the cloifters was the dormitory of the monks, divided into about forty cells.

In November, 1848, a great difcovery was made of the foundations of the Abbot's houfe, which was fituated to the fouth-eaft of the Lady Chapel, and alfo built on arches over

FOUNTAINS ABBEY. 145

the ruin. The falling in of part of thefe arches led to the
difcovery, and the foundations have fince been laid bare, and
prefent very interefting details of the goodly manfion of the
abbots, containing a fine pillared hall, one hundred and
feventy-one feet long by feventy feet wide, ample kitchens,
chapel, refectory, and a ftable for the fix white horfes which drew

FOUNTAINS : LADY CHAPEL.

the chariot of the laft abbot. "*Sex equi ad bigam.*" Amongft
the rubbifh which covered the foundations, were found many
ornamental encauftic tiles, and amongft the afhes of the
kitchen curious fragments of filver plate, pottery, etc., and

U

abundance of oyster, mussel, and cockle shells, showing the liberal use of fish by the holy brotherhood.

It appears that Sir Stephen Proctor, of Warfill, in 1611, pulled down this fine old abbot's house, to build himself a mansion, which still stands on a steep and wooded slope, at a short distance from the western gate of the abbey. The old house, with its large mullioned windows, its picturesque gables, its oddly out of keeping Ionic porch with sundial over it, its balcony, its statues, purloined from the abbey, and its clipped yew hedges, is an object well becoming the scene, though we should have preferred that Sir Stephen had found some other quarry for his stones than the abbot's dwelling.

The view of the buildings is beautiful as you stand at the south end of the Lady Chapel and take in the extent of the lofty walls and windows, one above another, with the trees beyond equalling them in height. The old rocks also, showing themselves along the north side of the abbey, overhung with trees which have grown since the abbey itself was hewn out of those rocks, are remarkably picturesque.

Near the abbey, on the other side of the river, which we cross by an old bridge, still stands the abbey mill, looking ancient and in excellent keeping with the scene. It still grinds for the people of the neighbourhood as it ground for the monks, and looks out dustily from amongst ancient trees. There is also a saw-mill hissing lustily as in modern contempt of all this antiquity. Near the old mill stands one of the most antiquated groups of yew-trees that eye ever beheld. There were probably seven of them, for they are still called the "Seven Sisters," though there are only three or four remaining, huge and hollow, but still most of them vigorous in foliage. One of them is twenty-five feet in circumference, and they are calculated to have stood here twelve centuries.

They have long outlived, not only the magnificent abbey, but the fyftem out of which it rofe. Long may they continue cafting the fpirit of long-paft ages over a fcene which combines the ever-living forms of nature fo lovingly with the fhattered remains of mediæval art, that together they feem rather a vifion of poetry than a reality of this matter-of-fact era. It is difficult, even while thefe graceful piles ftand before us amid the folemnity of ancient meadow, hill and wood, to conceive that they once were enfouled by a life fo oppofed to everything now moving around us. The world of monks walking in dim cloifters, and fending up their daily anthems amid fuch incenfed fhrines and arcades of foaring columns, and the world of railroads and bufy forges and populous factories, appear impoffible, as the growth of the fame ground and the fame minds. We can fcarcely do more than regard them as raifed to embody the dreams of poets, and to give a new charm to the fummer day's ramble, by fuch lapfing ftreams and through fuch fhadowy woodlands as thofe of Fountain dale.

Roslin Chapel and Castle.

HERE is no place in Scotland which fame for beauty and poetry has excited fo lively a defire in the tourift to fee, as Roflin and its neighbour Hawthornden; and the wifh is eafily gratified on the arrival at Edinburgh, for thefe celebrated fpots are only about feven miles to the fouth of that city. But great is the wonder of the traveller as he advances in that direction. He has not long quitted the romantic environs of the Scottifh capital, and begins with eagernefs to look a-head for this promifed fairyland, when he beholds only a plain, bald tract of country, over which are rolling the fmoke of coal-pit fires. The farther he goes the ftronger becomes his amazement. The black hills of coal-refufe; carts and wagons laden with that black but ufeful mineral pafs him, and he beholds a very ordinary country interfected by ftone walls, fcarred and disfigured by all the features of a coal-mining region; and with hundreds of engine-chimneys vomiting fmoke.

But anon he comes to the edge of a deep and narrow valley, at the bottom of which runs a rapid ftream, and the fteep banks of this glade are varied by every charm of rocks and woods, and dwellings of paft or prefent generations. Here ftands the far-famed chapel, worthy of all its reputation, there perched at the brink of the deep and fteep glen, the ruins of the ancient caftle, with a modern houfe erected amongft them; and there a little farther is the claffic abode of the poet Drummond; but far moft interefting of the whole, from its unique architecture, is the chapel. This was founded in 1446, a period of exuberant ornament in church architecture, and this has a character of its own, one in which the genius of building and carving feems to have revelled in its moft original mood.

The founder of Roflin Chapel was William de St. Clair, Earl of Orkney and Lord of Roflin, in the caftle of which he refided. He was a great man in his day, and fo far as we can judge from his acts, was a man not only held in high eftimation

ROSLIN CHAPEL, INTERIOR.

by his monarch, but one who had a mind far more liberal and judicious than his order and his rank were calculated to infpire. This is the account we find of him in Robertfon's Index :— " As admiral of the fleet, he conveyed the Princefs Margaret to France in 1436; he was Chancellor of Scotland from 1454 to 1458; he was made Earl of Caithnefs in 1455. In 1470 he refigned the earldom of Orkney to the king, and obtained in return various lands in Fife. Having, in 1459, fettled the barony of Newburgh, in Aberdeenfhire, on William, his only fon by his firft wife, Lady Margaret Douglas, he, in 1476, fettled the barony of Roflin, and his other eftates in Lothian, on Oliver St. Clair, his eldeft fon by his fecond marriage; and he transferred the earldom of Caithnefs to William, the fecond fon of his fecond marriage. The eminent founder of Roflin Chapel died foon after this fettlement, *which deranged his eftates, and degraded his family.*"

What a fingular derangement of his eftates in this great Earl St. Clair, by dividing them amongft his fons, inftead of heaping them, contrary to all the laws of nature and equity, on one! What a ftrange degradation of his family, by making them equal participants of his property! So pitiably do feudal inftitutions pervert the minds not only of poffeffors but of hiftorians.

In erecting this chapel, Earl William feems to have exercifed the fame breadth and originality of mind; for he chofe an architect of a brave and unique genius. Mr. Britton, in his " Architectural Antiquities of Great Britain," thus expreffes his perception of the fine and peculiar character of the ftyle :—
" This building, I believe, may be pronounced unique, and I am confident it will be found curious, elaborate, and fingularly interefting. The chapels of King's College, St. George, and Henry VIII., are all conformable to the ftyles of the

refpective ages when they were erected; and thefe ftyles difplay a gradual advancement in lightnefs and profufion of ornament; but the chapel of Roflin combines the folidity of the Norman with the minute decoration of the Tudor age. It is impoffible to defignate the architecture of this building by any given or familiar term; for the variety and eccentricity of its parts are not defined by any of common acceptation. I afk fome of our obftinate antiquaries, how they could apply either the term Roman, Saxon, Norman, Gothic, Saracenic, Englifh, or Grecian, to this building."

The founder intended to have erected it into a regular collegiate church, having a provoft, fix prebendaries, and two chorifters, or finging boys, and he endowed it with lands and revenues befitting; but he died when he had only completed the nave, which is the prefent chapel, and it was ufed as the chapel to the caftle. The hill on which he built it was called College Hill, and the people of the neighbourhood ftill call it the College. It ftands on the northern bank of the Efk. "Some additions," fays Chalmers in his "Account of North Britain," "were made to the endowment by fucceeding Barons of Roflin. In 1523, Sir William St. Clair granted fome lands in the vicinity of the chapel, for dwelling-houfes and gardens, and other accommodations to the provoft and prebendaries. In his charter, he mentions four altars in this chapel; one dedicated to St. Matthew, another to the Virgin, a third to St. Andrew, and a fourth to St. Peter. The commencement of the reformation by tumult, was the fignal for violence and fpoliation. The provoft and prebendaries of Roflin felt the effects of this fpirit. They were defpoiled of their revenues; and in 1572, they were compelled to relinquifh their whole property, which, indeed, had been withheld from them during many revolutionary years."

Beneath this chapel was the burial-place of the barons of Roflin; "fo dry," fays Slezer in 1693, "that the bodies at the end of eighty years were found in it entire." Ten barons had been buried there before the revolution; and of old, fays Hay, "they were buried in their armour without any coffin. The firft baron who was buried in a coffin was when the Duke of York, afterwards James II., was in Scotland. He and feveral antiquaries were oppofed to his having a coffin, but the widow infifted on it, declaring it to be beggarly to be buried without. The chapel," continues Hay, "of which any nation may be proud, was defaced by the fame ungoverned mob which pillaged the caftle of Roflin, on the night of the 11th of December, 1688." The caftle, after ftanding the fhocks of the reformation and the revolution, was at length refigned to time and chance. The chapel was repaired in the laft century by General St. Clair; and has fince been renovated by his fucceffors.

We may rejoice that, notwithftanding the affaults and perils through which this beautiful chapel has paffed, in common with almoft every ecclefiaftical building in Scotland, it remains fo entire as it does. It is a fpecimen of the ecclefiaftical architecture of Scotland that is without peer. Outfide and infide it is a truly beautiful object. Its ailes on each fide are fupported by rows of pointed arches, of which the pillars are not more than eight feet high, with cluftered fhafts of a maffivenefs equalling the Saxon; and the arches themfelves richly ornamented in fucceffive corded bands, or fpandrels. The capitals of the pillars are alfo elaborately carved in foliage intermingled with figures. One pillar has a renown of its own. It is called the *'prentice pillar*, the legend being that the apprentice of the architect executed this in his mafter's abfence, and when he returned and faw its furpaffing beauty, he knocked out the lad's brains with his hammer. The figure of the 'prentice is pointed out on the top of another pillar, and not far off is a buſt, ſaid to be that of his mother, who is looking at his dead body and weeping. The pillar is of exquiſite workmanſhip, being covered with the moſt delicate tracery, which runs ſpirally round it. Such a legend is not con-

ROSLIN : 'PRENTICE PILLAR.

fined to Roſlin; there is a 'prentice pillar in one of the churches at Rouen, and of a ſimilar nature is the legend of the celebrated aſtronomical clock in Straſburg Cathedral, that the inventor had no ſooner completed it than the corporation had his eyes put out, that he might not make another like it.

On the pavement of the chapel is the outline of one of the barons, lying in effigy, with a greyhound at his feet. Nothing is more common than for some animal, the chief cognizance of the family, to be thus placed at the feet of knight or baron. " But in this cafe," fays Robert Chambers, " it has given rife to a peculiar ftory, which is thus related to all vifitors by the perfon who now fhows the chapel. The perfon here delineated," he fays, " is Sir William de St. Clair. He was one day hunting over Roflin Moor along with King Robert Bruce, when a white deer was ftarted. Roflin wagered his head that his excellent hounds Hold and Help would feize the deer before it could crofs the March Burn. It was juft about to do fo, without being feized, when Roflin's emergency made him at once pious and poetical. He vowed a chapel to St. Katherine, provided fhe would take his cafe in hand, and fhouted out to the foremoft of his dogs :—

'Help, haud, an' ye may,
Or Roflin will lose his head this day.'

Help, affifted by the faint, and encouraged by her mafter, made a defperate leap forward, and pulled down the deer juft as it was about to leap upon land. The baron, too much terrified by the rifk to enjoy the efcape, immediately put his foot upon the dog's neck, and killed it, faying it fhould never again lead him into fuch temptation." It ufed to be a belief in the neighbourhood that, on the night before any of the barons died, the whole of the chapel appeared in flames. In 1805, the Marchionefs of Stafford took fome fketches of Roflin Chapel, which were etched in 1807, and circulated in a fmall volume amongft her friends.

Roflin Caftle, overhanging the picturefque glen of the Efk, is, as we have faid, a ruin, with a modern houfe built in the midft of it; but the three lower ftories, being below the level of the fummit of the bank, are yet entire. A beautiful Scottifh fong, bearing its name, has connected its memory with the public mind, far and wide.

ROSLIN CASTLE.

[By Richard Hewitt, a native of Cumberland, who acted as conductor to Dr. Blacklock, the blind Scottifh poet, and died in 1764. It is always included among the Scottifh fongs. The air is Scotch, and very beautiful.]

'Twas in that feafon of the year,
When all things gay and fweet appear,
That Colin, with the morning ray,
Arofe and fung his rural lay.
Of Nancy's charms the fhepherd fung,
The hills and dales with Nancy rung,
While Roflin Caftle heard the fwain,
And echoed back the cheerful ftrain.

Awake, fweet Mufe! the breathing fpring
With rapture warms; awake and fing!
Awake and join the rural throng,
Who hail the morning with a fong:
To Nancy raife the cheerful lay,
O! bid her hafte and come away;
In fweeteft fmiles herfelf adorn,
And add new graces to the morn.

O! hark, my love, on every fpray
Each feathered warbler tunes his lay,
'Tis beauty fires the ravifhed throng,
And love infpires the melting fong;
Then let my raptured notes arife,
For beauty darts from Nancy's eyes,
And love my rifing bofom warms,
And fills my foul with fweet alarms.

O! come, my love; thy Colin's lay
With rapture calls—O! come away!
Come while the mufe this wreath fhall twine
Around that modeft brow of thine:
O! hither hafte, and with thee bring
That beauty blooming like the fpring,
Thofe graces that divinely fhine,
And charm this ravifhed breaft of mine!

It would leave but a very imperfect idea of Roflin and its locality, did we omit to mention that near it ftands Hawthornden, the houfe of the poet Drummond, the friend of Shakspeare and Ben Jonfon. We believe the place is ftill in the poffeffion of a defcendant of the family. It ftands on a precipitous rock overhanging the fouth bank of the river. We cannot do better than tranfcribe the account of it given by Robert Chambers, in his "Picture of Scotland."

"Hawthornden may be defcribed as a manor-houfe of the reign of Charles I., engrafted on the ruins of an ancient baronial caftle. On one fide its walls rife directly from the brink of a deep precipice; on the other, they adjoin to a level and well-cultivated domain. The walks around the houfe are peculiarly fine, being chiefly laid throughout the beautiful vale of the Efk. Admiffion to them can only be obtained by an order from the proprietor.

"What muft add greatly to the charm of Hawthornden, is, that the prefent houfe was built by the poet: as is teftified by an infcription on the front. Many of the minor localities around the houfe are affociated with his name; as an arbour where he ufed to fit at his long daily mufings, and a fummer-houfe where he is faid to have often taken his food. But perhaps the moft interefting of all the neighbouring objects, is a large tree near the place where the external gate of the court-yard formerly ftood—a tree which feems to have acted the part of the Covin tree. This Covin or Coglin tree ftood in front of old manfion-houfes in Scotland, and to it the hoft attended his guefts bare-headed on their departure.

"Ben Jonfon, it is generally known, walked all the way from London on foot to fee Drummond at this his paternal refidence. Regarding this vifit, tradition records a circumftance fo characteriftic and fo probable, that I can not but believe it true. Drummond, it is faid, on feeing Ben approaching the houfe, went out, like a good landlord, to the outfide of his gate, in order to bid him welcome, according to form, under the fhade of this tree. As he fhook the dramatift by the hand, he exclaimed in mock-heroic ftyle :—

"Welcome, welcome, royal Ben."

To which Jonfon immediately anfwered in fuch a way as to make up a Hudibraftic couplet :—

"Thank ye, thank ye, Hawthornden!"

"The two poets enjoyed the pleafure of each other's converfation for a confiderable time ; and the ftranger will fcarcely vifit without confiderable emotion the place where, in the words of Collins—

"Jonfon fat in Drummond's claffic fhade."

"It is melancholy to add, that the vifit of Jonfon to Drummond refulted in a violent quarrel and eftrangement. Jonfon during his fojourn at Hawthornden, opened his heart to the poet, and talked freely of his contemporaries in London. All this was in the confidence of friendfhip, but it was greedily drunk in by Drummond, and daily or nightly carefully written down. Some time after, Jonfon, to his great aftonifhment and indignation, found the whole given to the world by his treacherous hoft in his notorious 'Converfations.' The anger and reproaches of Ben were as pungent and unfparing as they were juftly merited by the falfe country poet. We wifh we could fay that this habit of noting down confidential converfations, and *confiding* them to the whole world through the prefs, were confined to the time of Jonfon and the laird of Hawthornden ; and that fome ready penmen of the prefent day would be able to caft a ftone at Drummond with a clear confcience.

" Several detached curiosities are shown to strangers in the inside of Hawthornden House: as, for instance, the walking-cane of the celebrated Duchess of Lauderdale, a stately old piece of timber with a pike at one end and a crook at the other, communicating—unless fancy has strangely deceived the present writer—a striking idea of the personal bearing of that most singular lady. There are also a number of family portraits, including a fine queen Mary.

" In the face of the precipice upon which Hawthornden is reared, the stranger, in traversing the glen, sees a number of holes. These are the orifices of a singular suite of caverns which penetrate the rock beneath the house. No stranger omits seeing this singular curiosity. In the court-yard he is first shown a well of prodigious depth, which communicates with the caves. He then descends a narrow stair to a long subterranean passage, on each side of which there are small apartments, much after the fashion of a suite of bed-rooms in an old house. Below this there is what may be called a lower story, which also contains rooms, and, the passage of which looks out upon the glen at one of the holes mentioned. The shaft of the well communicates with another end of this passage; so that the inmates of these caves could not only draw up their own water when they pleased, but also be supplied with food by their friends above, by means of a bucket.

" Without adverting to the circumstance that these caverns must have been originally formed by the early Britons, whose molelike preference of darkness to light in their fortified residences is a fact very well known to antiquaries; it may be mentioned that, by the invariable tradition of the country, they afforded shelter to the distressed friends of Bruce, if not to that hero himself, at a time when they dared not show their faces above-ground. In one of the apartments a recess is shown, which is said to have contained the bed used by the heroic

Edward Bruce, brother to the king, during his refidence here. In the fucceeding age they are faid to have been ufed for the fame purpofe by Sir Alexander Ramfay, the knight who flew man and horfe, and broke the pavement-ftone in Candle-maker Row,—and by his hardy band of compatriots, who nightly fallied forth from this hiding-place to annoy their enemies, and who thus invariably efcaped detection."

The poetry of Drummond, though much praifed in his time, is not of a character to pleafe ours. Much of it confifts of occafional verfes "On a Parrot," or "To his Miftrefs's Eyebrow," or, at leaft, verfes of that ftamp. Others are well worded, but deftitute of living fentiment; while fome are extremely obfcene. In fact, the bulk of his compofitions refemble a vaft mafs of others ftored in our libraries, which would be better in bonfires to make room for better things. His poems of devotion, the beft part of his writings, do not warm us: they will not do after Herbert, Cowper, Keble, and Montgomery. This fonnet is the only thing bearing any reference to Hawthornden, where he fpent fo much of his life, and wrote moft of his verfe:—

SONNET.

"Dear wood, and you, fweet folitary place,
Where from the vulgar I eftrangèd live,
Contented more with what your fhades me give,
Than if I had what Thetis doth embrace;
What fnaky eye, grown jealous of my peace,
Now from your filent horrors would me drive,
When fun, progreffing in his glorious race
Beyond the Twins, doth near our pole arrive?
What fweet delight a quiet life affords,
And what it is to be of bondage free,
Far from the madding worldling's hoarfe difcords,
Sweet flowery place, I firft did learn of thee:
Ah! if I were mine own, your dear reforts
I would not change with princes' ftately courts."

We are ſorry to hear that there is a proceſs of ſo-called renovating going on in this beautiful chapel, by ſharpening up its ſculptures. We muſt ſay that we prefer the original cutting, though it may be ſomewhat worn by time, and have a natural ſhrinking at the idea of touching up what we prefer ſeeing to be old, rather than to be vainly perſuaded by modern chiſels that it is new.

Elgin Cathedral.

> Time hath not wronged her, nor hath ruin fought
> Rudely her fplendid ftructures to deftroy,
> Save in thofe recent days, with evil fraught,
> When mutability, in drunken joy
> Triumphant, and from all reftraint releafed,
> Let loofe her fierce and many-headed beaft.
>
> SOUTHEY.

 HE ancient capital of Morayfhire ftretches along its level fite a few miles from where the Spey falls into the ocean, in a grey and ftately antiquity that fpeaks of better days. Changes of life and manners have led away the landed gentry to fouthern cities, and their old abodes ftand, bearing on their venerable fronts their names, and the dates of their erection, but now devolved to more plebeian occupation. Changes of faith have alfo rent down that noble fane, once the nobleft of all Scotland. The cathedral was originally built in the early part of the thirteenth century, a period at which arofe fo many of the ecclefiaftical fabrics of both England and Scotland. But this firft church was deftroyed by fire in 1390, by one of the moft rude and fierce of Scotland's old ariftocracy. Alexander Stuart, the fon of Robert II., king of Scotland, a man properly

Y

called the Wolf of Badenoch, having a feud with Bifhop Barr, burnt down the cathedral, the parifh church, a religious houfe called Maifon Dieu, eighteen houfes of the canons, and the greateft part of the city. He was compelled for this offence to do penance before the high altar of Blackfriars' Church at Perth : a very flight punifhment for fuch an offence. The city did not recover its previous condition for a long time ; and it was many years before the new cathedral was completed. The bifhops devoted a third of their incomes to this object, and at length it ftood a church of rare beauty and fplendour. Its central tower was one hundred and ninety-eight feet high,

ELGIN CATHEDRAL ; SOUTH AISLE.

and the prefent remains juftify the character which it attained of being the fineft fpecimen of ecclefiaftical architecture in the kingdom, Melrofe not excepted. It exceeds that admired fabric in extent, in altitude, in general magnificence, and in richnefs of decoration. The remains of it at the prefent day are beheld by ftrangers with equal wonder and pleafure.

This fine cathedral, like nearly all in Scotland, fell, not by time, but by the fierce and bigoted fpirit in which the reformation was introduced. In 1568, the privy council authorifed the Earl of Huntley, the fheriff of Aberdeen, to ftrip the cathedral churches of Aberdeen and Elgin of their lead, and to fell it for the maintenance of the troops of the regent Murray. It is a curious fact that this plunder, like the lead ftripped from the caftle of Conway in Wales, was not deftined to benefit the fpoilers. As that was loft with the fhip which was conveying it to Ireland, fo this had fcarcely left the harbour of Aberdeen for Holland, where it was to be fold, when the fhip went down with it. The cathedral of Elgin, thus expofed to the elements, went gradually to decay, and in 1711 the great central tower fell.

Wordfworth fpeaking of fuch rude and felfifh deftruction of ancient churches from a probably juft refentment againft the evils and oppreffions of a corrupted faith, fays :—

> " As when a ftorm hath ceafed, the birds regain
> Their cheerfulnefs, and bufily retrim
> Their nefts, or chant a gratulating hymn,
> To the blue ether and befpangled plain ;
> Even fo, in many a reconftructed fane,
> Have the furvivors of this ftorm renewed
> Their holy rites with vocal gratitude :
> And folemn ceremonials they ordain
> To celebrate their great deliverance ;
> Moft feelingly inftructed 'mid their fear,

> That perfecution, blind with rage extreme,
> May not the lefs, through heaven's mild countenance
> Even in her own defpite, both feed and cheer;
> For all things are lefs dreadful than they feem."

But no fuch fecond refurrection awaited this fuperb old temple. The fpirit of Genevan aufterity, which came over with John Knox, allowed no revival of papal grandeur, but inaugurated a clafs of houfes of devotion of a more rigid fimplicity.

The parts of the dilapidated cathedral remaining moft entire are, the eaft end, parts of the tranfepts, the chapter-houfe, and the weftern entrance, flanked by two ftupendous towers. The workmanfhip of all thefe is of extraordinary richnefs and elaboratenefs. The weftern door is particularly fine, and the chapter-houfe will bear comparifon with moft of thofe generally elegant buildings. Many monuments remain and are now guarded with care. Some of the figures reprefent knights and barons lying in complete armour, and others are of bifhops, of a coloffal fize. The furrounding area is the parifh burial-ground, which is enclofed by a high wall, and kept fhut up with the care fo characteriftic of the Scotch in their cemeteries.

Connected with the ruins of this cathedral is a hiftory which is curious. The free fchool of the town, which provides clothing and maintenance for fuch children as cannot be fupported by their parents, is a modern foundation. " It owes its origin," fays Robert Chambers, in his " Picture of Scotland," " to a native of Elgin, who, having made a fortune abroad, devoted his honourable earnings to this honourable purpofe. His name was Andrew Anderfon, a major-general in the fervice of the Eaft India Company; and there is fomething fingular in his hiftory. He contrived to raife himfelf from the condition of a private foldier to that honourable rank, entirely by his own merits. He had no patrimony but genius and ambition; there was fomething even below poverty in his origin. A fmall apartment is fhown amid the ruins of the cathedral, where his mother, an indigent and infirm old widow, who could afford no better lodging, lived for many years while he was a

ELGIN CATHEDRAL: CHOIR.

boy; and this I humbly conceive to be, in one fenfe, the greateft curiofity about Elgin. In a crib, not more than five feet fquare, furrounded by melancholy ruins, and the dread-infpiring precinéts of a churchyard, Anderfon fpent all his early years; the boy, who was on this account, perhaps, the moſt wretched and defpifed of all the boys in the town, being all the time deſtined to reach fuperior honours, and make provifion for numbers of fuch outcaſts as himfelf. Let the ſtranger inquire for, enter, and ponder upon, this humble cradle of genius and greatnefs."

Holyrood Abbey and Palace.

HE abbey and palace of Holyrood, though connected and long alike ufed for royal purpofes, are of very different dates and in very different conditions. The abbey is ancient, and is now reduced to the mere ruins of the nave of the church, which, as you face the palace, is joined to the pofterior angle of that building on the left hand. The palace is ftill complete, yet it is of two very diftinct dates. It is built round a quadrangle, the back and fides of which are comparatively modern, for in 1544 the palace was burnt down by the Englifh. The front alone would feem to have efcaped ; or, rather, only the double towers at each corner of the front. Thefe have an antique look, being round, projecting, machicolated, battlemented, and furmounted by fmaller lantern towers. The façade betwixt thefe is a plain Grecian fcreen of one ftory, having a central gateway furmounted by a dome. The other three fides of the quadrangle are of plain building, of two ftories, and an attic, fhown by its dormer-windows, all round.

Thefe royal buildings are fituated at the fouth-eaft of Edinburgh, and therefore, contrary to London, do not conftitute a Weft-End. In fact, they are very much crowded upon by the worft part of the city, though furrounded by fine hills ; as Calton Hill on one fide and Arthur's Seat in the old park on the other. The abbey having been anciently a fanctuary, the vicinity of the palace has continued to this time a fanctuary for debtors, who are fecure from the law within a certain circuit.

The abbey was founded by David I., who was famous for his piety, and, having been a refident at the court of Henry I. of England, had feen how much was there doing for the church by fuch foundations. It was built early in the twelfth century, and David fent to St. Andrew's for a number of canons regular to inhabit it. It foon became rich by fucceffive endowments of lands and churches in different counties. In the ancient *Taxatio* the lands of this abbey, which was called Holycrofs or Holyrood, were valued at £88. The abbot and canons posfeffed equal privileges with the bifhop of St. Andrews, or the abbots of Dunfermline or Kelfo. They were authorized to build a fuburb adjoining Edinburgh, and hence arofe the ancient Canongate, and the Girth-Crofs at the foot of the Canongate marked the limits of the fanctuary.

The following are the leading events connected with this religious houfe. It was plundered by Edward II.'s army when it retired from Lothian in Auguft, 1332. Edward Baliol held his parliament in the abbey in February, 1333-4. The Duke of Lancafter in 1381 was hofpitably entertained in the abbey while feeking refuge in Scotland. Richard II. in his furious inroad in Scotland in 1385, burnt it down. Henry IV. fpared the abbey during his invafion in 1400, becaufe his father had found refuge in it. The different Scottifh kings, though refiding chiefly in the caftle perched on its noble rock at the other extremity of Edinburgh, frequently paffed much time in the abbey. The queen of James I. of Scotland was delivered of twins in the abbey ; and James II., one of thefe twins, was crowned in it in 1427. He was married in it in 1449 to Mary of Guelder, and he was buried in it in 1460. Thus James II.

was born, crowned, married, and buried in the abbey of Holyrood. James III., whenever he refided in Edinburgh, took up his quarters in the abbey. James IV. was the builder of the palace, for the Scottifh monarchs feem greatly to have preferred its fheltered fituation to the expofed one of the caftle. This muft have been not later than 1500, for here in 1503, he received

HOLYROOD ABBEY; INTERIOR.

Margaret of England, and here they were married. In 1544, the abbey and palace were burnt by the Englifh army: this, however, muft have been with exception of the towers in front. From this time the abbey church feems to have become the chapel of the palace—a chaplain being maintained

z

by the king to officiate for the royal family. After the battle of Pinkie, September, 1547, Protector Somerset sent two commissioners, Boham and Chamberlayne, to suppress the monastery of Holyrood. They found the monks already fled, but they stripped the abbey of the lead, and carried off the two bells; one of which was afterwards hung in the chapel of the Cowgate, built for the English communion in 1771. The reformers in June 1559 further spoiled the abbey, and damaged the palace also. The unfortunate Queen Mary was married in the abbey church to Lord Darnley on the 29th of July, 1566; and on the 15th of May, 1567, she was again married to the Earl of Bothwell in the hall of the palace. Again, on the imprisonment of Mary in 1567, that is, in the same year as her second marriage, the Earl of Glencairn ransacked the chapel of Holyrood House. At the suppression of the abbey it enjoyed a greater revenue than any other religious house of the southern shires of Scotland. This revenue was in money £2,926 8s. 6d., besides one paid annually in kind, of thirty-six chalders ten bolls of wheat, forty chalders nine bolls of barley, thirty-four chalders sixteen bolls of oats, four chalders of meal, five hundred and one capons, twenty-four hens, twenty-four salmon, three swine, and ten loads of salt: a most magnificent revenue in Scotland at that period.

After the suppression of the monastery, the abbey church was used as the parish church of the Cowgate; but James the Sixth of Scotland and First of England,—the British Solomon,—sent workmen from London to repair and beautify it, but unfortunately he ordered the portraits of the apostles to be painted on the walls. At this the Genevan spirit of the Scotch reformers took fire; they declared that no " graven images " should be set up there, and James was advised by the dean of the chapel, the Bishop of Galloway, as he valued his peace to desist, which he did, only lamenting that prejudice could not diftinguifh betwixt ornament and image. Charles II., after his reftoration, appropriated the church of the abbey as the chapel royal; and had it handfomely fitted up for the fovereign and the knights of the Order of the Thiftle, to whom the key of the church was configned. He alfo erected an organ in it. The chapel was finally ruined at the revolution, by attempting to put a ftone roof on it, which proved too heavy for the walls, and it fell, demolifhing the whole interior. Since then it has remained a ruin. Charles II. alfo had the palace rebuilt by Sir William Bruce, and this is the date of the main portion of the building.

The chief events connected with the palace, befides thofe enumerated, belong to the reign of the unfortunate Mary. In her time the building of the palace was modern, and fhe occupied it during her fhort and troubled reign with much fplendour. In it fhe witneffed fome moft dreadful and moft miferable tranfactions, and the intereft and romance of her forrowful life are thofe which ftill more than all others envelope it.

For many ages the monarchs of England had been determined on the annexation of Scotland by arms, as they had annexed Wales and Ireland. But, difappointed in this, no fooner was James V. dead, leaving only a daughter, a week old, to fucceed him, than Henry VIII. determined on fecuring the union of this kingdom by the marriage of this daughter with his fon Edward. Events defeated his defign; Mary was married to the French dauphin, and became Queen of France by her hufband's acceffion to the crown as Francis II. During her abode in France, Scotland was governed by her mother, Mary of Guife, as queen-regent. But fhe had a terrible time of it; Scotland being repeatedly invaded by the armies of Elizabeth of England; and, still worse, the whole of the Scotch nobles being bought up by her money. Henry VIII. had commenced this system when he had failed, by his arbitrary impatience, to secure the young queen for his son. He had invaded and ravaged the country to seize her, and afterwards to avenge himself for his failure. He then sent commissioners to Berwick to bribe the nobles, and instigated them to murder the cardinal Beaton, in order to put down the Catholic party, who were vehemently opposed to him as the great enemy of their church. The documents of his reign and of the succeeding reigns of his son and two daughters, which have been printed in our time by order of Parliament, have laid open to the world the whole of this system of murder and bribery by the Tudors; and surely there is in history scarcely any other such revelation of horror and wickedness recorded by the hands of the actors themselves. We have the correspondence for the murder of Beaton with the nobles, who refused to do that detestable act, but only because they could not obtain a written order from the King for the commission of it; Sir Ralph Saddler, Henry's commissioner of murder at Berwick, informing them that the king's honour must be saved. He then employed Norman Leslie, who executed it, and we have his letter informing Saddler that it was done, and asking what he should do next. Elizabeth maintained this system, and the whole of her dark transactions remain under the hands of her ministers Walsingham, Cecil, Randolph, Saddler, and others. Never surely had so wicked a queen a knot of such cold-blooded and desperately wicked ministers! And yet how little could they be aware of the intense infamy of their conduct; or they would have destroyed those proofs of it which have been brought forth from our national archives, and published by authority of government in our day.

By the syftem there revealed in incontrovertible and imperishable characters, Mary of Scotland, from the hour of her birth, was enveloped in a web of English policy and of Scotch treason, fine as a cobweb, but infrangible as a net of steel! When she returned, a young and beautiful widow of seventeen, full of wit and knowledge and accomplishment, she came home into the midst of a nobility, not only rude and ferocious beyond any other in Europe, but all in the pay of Elizabeth of England. She came amongst a desperate set of traitors fee'd for her destruction, and the more prompt to it from being the greater part of them proselytes of Knox and of the Genevan faith,—a faith which had more of the old leaven of the vengeance of Judaism than of the love and mercy of Christ. It was in this palace of Holyrood that Mary was hunted down, bearded and insulted, by Knox, and her own base brother, the Earl of Murray; by the steel-clad and steel-hearted nobles, Morton, Lethington, Ruthven, and the rest of them. Here it was that they incited her husband Darnley with jealous rage to assist them in murdering her secretary and musician, Rizzio, in her presence, in 1556. By them Bothwell was instigated to murder her husband, Earl Darnley, in February, 1567; and by their machinations Mary was carried off by Bothwell, and compelled to marry him in May of the same year. By these means the fame of Mary was irrevocably ruined with her people, and the ends of Elizabeth so far gained. The most audacious forgeries were committed by the English minister Cecil and his agents, both of state documents and of pretended love-letters of Mary to Bothwell. The details and proofs of these matters are too voluminous for these pages, but they stand broadly displayed in the official publication referred to. George Chalmers also, in his "Caledonia," (vol. ii., quarto,) says, "When the heart and hand of forgery are busy in any age, it is not eafy to afcertain falfehood from truth. We fee in Haynes the fucceffive intimations of Cecil, while his artful mind was bufily employed at Edinburgh, in carrying on a double negotiation, with whatever view of gratifying his paffion for intrigue, or benefiting his faftidious miftrefs. What was given by the infurgent chiefs to Cecil, and by him after a while, or by his direction, was depofited in the Cotton Library, has long been publifhed; and what has thus been obtruded on the world as genuine, and has been reprobated as fpurious, need not be elaborately inveftigated, as the envoys had no power to negotiate with the infurgents." He adds, "The memory of Cecil alfo is chargeable with an additional offence of aggravated bafenefs:—by filling the archives of England with forgeries, he has contaminated the fountain-head of hiftory." (P. 637.)

Whitaker, Tyler, and others, have expofed at large thefe dark tranfactions. By them Mary, hunted down into the toils of Elizabeth, and trufting to her honour and hofpitality, entered her kingdom, only to be made the tenant of a dungeon for eighteen years, and then put to death. No time can wafh away the fable ftains of thefe crimes from the memory of Henry VIII. and of Elizabeth, nor from the honour of England. No Froude can by any arts of fophiftry wafh thefe royal blackamoors white. It is worthy of remark that, according to the parliamentary hiftory of Scotland, Mary, ftaunch Catholic as fhe was, has the honour of having, in the parliament of 1567, paffed the very firft act of religious toleration known in the Chriftian world. In the Parliamentary Record (p. 752,) we find that in April, 1567, "the queen, with the advice of the three Eftates, repealed all former acts which impofed any penalty on the religion thus exifting within her realm. And, with the advice of the three Eftates, the queen declared herself the head and protector of the church, in opposition *to all foreign authority*, power and jurisdiction, whether ecclesiastical or temporal."

"In this manner then," says Chalmers, (vol. ii., p. 657,) "do the Roman Catholic Mary Stuart, and the Parliament of April, 1567, enjoy the unrivalled honour of being the earliest legislators, within the British islands, who passed *an act of toleration*, upon the purest principles of indulgence to conscience, and regard to freedom." Keith (p. 379,) declares this act to be full and explicit, for the settlement of the new religion; and Robertson (vol. i., p. 382,) concurs with Keith. It is true that this act was as repugnant to the feelings of stern and bigoted reformers of the time, who detested toleration, as it could be to the most bigoted Catholics. What a contrast to the intolerance of Henry VIII. and of Queen Elizabeth, who would allow no one to avow opinions different to their own! However much Mary Stuart may have sinned in her conduct, there is no question that she was infinitely more sinned against, and that her liberality in point of toleration of opposing faiths stands in noble contrast with the spirit of her persecutors. It is these facts, looking forth from beneath the accumulated calumnies heaped upon her memory by the powerful court of England, and by the tongues and pens of the able but unprincipled men who surrounded the British queen, which give such a deathless freshness to the memory of the Queen of Scots, and cause such numbers to walk the chambers of the venerable Holyrood with sadly sympathizing souls.

The following poem, by Wordsworth, supposed to be uttered by Queen Mary in her captivity, is a fair exponent of the popular sentiment towards her:—

Lament of
MARY QUEEN OF SCOTS
ON THE EVE OF A NEW YEAR.

" Smile of the moon ! for so I name
    That silent greeting from above ;
A gentle flash of light that came
    From her whom drooping captives love ;
Or art thou of still higher birth ?
Thou that didst part the clouds of earth
    My torpor to reprove !

" Bright boon of pitying heaven—alas !
    I may not trust thy placid cheer !
Pondering that Time to-night will pass
    The threshold of another year ;
For years to me are sad and dull ;
My very moments are too full
    Of hopelessness and fear.

" And yet, the soul-awakening gleam,
    That struck perchance the farthest cone
Of Scotland's rocky wilds, did seem
    To visit me, and me alone ;
Me, unapproached by any friend,
Save those who to my sorrow lend
    Tears due unto their own.

" To-night, the church-tower bells will ring
    Through these wide realms a festive peal ;
To the new year a welcoming ;
    A tuneful offering for the weal
Of happy millions lulled in sleep ;
While I am forced to watch and weep,
    By wounds that may not heal.

" Born all too high, by wedlock raised
    Still higher—to be cast thus low !
Would that mine eyes had never gazed
    On aught of more ambitious show,
Than the sweet flowerets of the fields !
— It is my royal state that yields
    This bitterness of woe.

"Yet how?—for I, if there be truth
　In the world's voice, was paſſing fair;
And beauty for confiding youth
　Thoſe ſhocks of paſſion can prepare,
That kill the bloom before its time,
And blanch without the owner's crime
　The moſt reſplendent hair.

"Unbleſt diſtinction! ſhowered on me,
　To bind a lingering life in chains;
All that could quit my graſp, or flee,
　Is gone; but not the ſubtle ſtains
Fixed in the ſpirit; for even here
Can I be proud that jealous fear
　Of what I was remains.

"A woman rules my priſon's key;
　A ſiſter queen, againſt the bent
Of law and holieſt ſympathy,
　Detains me—doubtful of th' event;
Great God, who feel'ſt for my diſtreſs,
My thoughts are all that I poſſeſs,
　O keep them innocent!

"Farewell deſire of human aid,
　Which abject mortals vainly court,
By friends deceived, by foes betrayed,
　Of fears the prey, of hopes the ſport;
Nought but the world-redeeming Croſs
Is able to ſupply my loſs,
　My burthen to support."

Hark! the death-note of the year
　Sounded by the caſtle clock.
From her ſunk eyes a ſtagnant tear
　Stole forth, unſettled by the ſhock;
But oft the woods renewed their green,
Ere the tired head of Scotland's Queen
　Reposed upon the block!

Since Holyrood Palace, by the Act of Union, has been made the place of meeting for the election of the noblemen who repreſent the peerage of Scotland in the Imperial Parliament, it has been, at different times, yet only for ſhort periods, inhabited by the Duke of York, afterwards James II. ; by Prince Charles Stuart; by the Duke of Cumberland; by the King of France from 1795 to 1799; by George IV. on his visit to Edinburgh in 1822; and by Queen Victoria on her annual journeys to Balmoral in the Highlands. For this purpose a certain suite of rooms, on the south side of the quadrangle, is fitted up. The rooms on the north side, a hundred and fifty feet in length, contain a long series of portraits of the Scotch monarchs, most of which are as fictitious as they are miserable. Many of them, indeed, are of personages who existed before the pictorial art existed in Scotland. There is also an indifferent Queen of Scots. In the room where Rizzio was murdered, you are still shown the traditional stains of his blood; and the apartments inhabited by Mary still contain furniture said to have been in use by her, as well as certain tapestry and embroidery, reported to be the work of herself and her ladies.

Melrose Abbey.

Summer was on thee—the meridian light—
    And, as we wandered through thy columned ailes,
    Decked all thy hoar magnificence with smiles,
Making the rugged soft, the gloomy bright ;
Nor was reflection from my heart apart,
    As clomb our steps the lone and lofty stair,
    Till gained the summit, ticked in silent air
Thine ancient clock, as 'twere thy throbbing heart :
Monastic grandeur and baronial pride
    Subdued, the former half, the latter quite,
    Pile of King David, to thine altar's site,
Full many a footstep guides and long shall guide ;
    Where those are met, who met not save in fight,
And Douglas sleeps with Evers, side by side.
            DAVID MACBETH MOIR.

HE foundation of Melrose Abbey generally dates from 1136, when David I. of Scotland, amongst his many similar erections, built a church here. But Melrose, as a seat of religion, boasts a much earlier origin. It was one of those churches, or more properly missionary stations, which the fathers of Ireland and of Iona spread over Britain and the continent: one of those simple nuclei of the Christian faith, which were in the eleventh and twelfth centuries so industriously trodden under foot or rooted out by the domineering ambition of Rome. It was in fact a portion of that pure and beautiful British church

which exifted prior to the Roman hierarchy in thefe iflands, and of which the profeffors prefented in their primitive habits and primitive doctrines fo apoftolic a character.

The way in which thefe apoftles of Iona were introduced into this quarter is thus related by Venerable Bede:—" As foon as Ofwald, the King of Northumberland, afcended the throne, being defirous that his nation fhould receive the Chriftian faith, whereof he had found happy experience in vanquifhing the barbarians, he fent to the elders of the Scots (Irifh), amongft whom himfelf and followers, when in banifhment, had received the facrament of baptifm, defiring that they would fend him a bifhop, by whofe inftruction and miniftry the Englifh nation, which he governed, might be taught the advantages and receive the facraments of the Chriftian faith. Nor were they flow in granting his requeft, but fent him Bifhop Aidan, a man of fingular meeknefs, piety, and moderation; zealous in the caufe of God, though not according to knowledge, for he was wont to keep Eafter Sunday according to the cuftom of his country, which we have before fo often mentioned—from the fourteenth to the twentieth moon,—the northern province of the Scots, and all the nation of the Picts, celebrated Eafter then after that manner, and believing that they were following the writings of the holy and praifeworthy Father Anatolius, the truth of which every fkilful perfon can difcern; but the Scots which dwelt in the fouth of Ireland had long fince, by the admonition of the bifhop of the Apoftolic fee, learned to obferve Eafter according to the canonical cuftom.

" On the arrival of the bifhop, the king appointed him his epifcopal fee in the ifle of Lindisfarn, as he defired, which place, as the tide flows and ebbs twice a-day, is enclofed by the waves of the fea like an ifland, and again twice in the day

MELROSE: FROM THE SOUTH-WEST.

when the ſhore is left dry, become contiguous to the land. The king alſo, humbly and willingly in all caſes giving ear to his admoniſhers, induſtriouſly applied himſelf to build and extend the Church of Chriſt in his kingdom, wherein, when the biſhop, not being ſkilful in the Engliſh tongue, preached the goſpel, it was moſt delightful to ſee the king himſelf interpreting the Word of God to his commanders and miniſtry, for he had perfectly learned the language of the Scots during his long baniſhment. From that time many of the Scots came daily into Britain, and with great devotion preached the Word to thofe provinces of the Englifh over which King Ofwald reigned, and thofe amongft them who had received priefts' orders, and miniftered to them the grace of baptifm. Churches were built in feveral places; and the people flocked joyfully together to hear the Word: money and lands were given of the king's bounty to build monafteries; the Englifh, great and fmall, were by their Scottifh mafters inftructed in the rules and obfervances of regular difcipline, for moft of them that came to preach were monks. Bifhop Aidan was himfelf a monk of the ifland of Hii (the ancient name of Iona), whofe monaftery was for a long time the chief of moft of thofe of the northern Scots, and of all thofe of the Picts, and had the direction of their people. That ifland belongs to Britain, being divided from it by a fmall arm of the fea; but had been long fince given by the Picts, who inhabit thofe parts of Britain, to the Scottifh monks, becaufe they had received the faith of Chrift through their preaching."

We are likewife told a very interefting fact regarding the coming of Aidan to Northumberland. At firft, in accordance with the requeft of King Ofwald, Corman, a pious but auftere monk, had been fent. He foon returned difpirited to Iona, faying, "The people to whom you fent me are fo obftinate that we muft renounce all idea of changing their manners." As Aidan heard this, he faid to himfelf, "O my Saviour! if thy love had been offered to this people, many hearts could have been touched. I will go and make thee known,—Thee who broke not the bruifed reed." Then turning to Corman, he faid, "Brother, you have been too fevere towards hearers fo dull of heart. You fhould have given them fpiritual milk to drink until they were able to receive more folid food." All eyes were fixed on the man who fpoke fo wifely. The brethren of Iona exclaimed, "Aidan is worthy of the epifcopate!" And accordingly he was confecrated by the laying on of the hands of the elders, and fent forth.

"From Lindisfarn," fays Bede, "Aidan travelled all around to fpread the gofpel. He was wont to traverfe both town and country on foot. The king gave him a fine horfe,—he foon gave it to a man in great need of one." Such is the teftimony of Bede to a teacher of doctrines oppofed to his own. One of the firſt churches planted muſt have been Melrofe; for Aidan only arrived in Northumberland in 635, and fixteen years afterwards there was a religious houfe there. The Iona apoftles continued biſhops of Lindisfarn till 664, during which time Finan and Colman had fucceeded Aidan. In Colman's time popery had reared a determined and fuccefsful champion in Wilfrid, Archbiſhop of York, who was favoured by Ofwy, who had now fucceeded King Ofwald. In that year (664) a grand conference was held at Whitby on the fubject of the differences of the two churches. On the one fide ſtood Colman, with the biſhops and elders of the Britons; on the other Biſhops Wilfrid and Agilbert, with many other prieſts and abbots, Hilda, abbefs of Whitby, and Cedder, an Engliſh biſhop who had gone over to Rome. The decifion was adverfe to the Iona creed, and rather than renounce it Colman and his brethren returned to Iona. The queſtion was not merely regarding the keeping of Eaſter and the peculiar ſhape of the tonfure, but the fupremacy of Rome, which the Iriſh clergy would not admit.

At this time we find that Eata,—one of twelve boys whom Aidan had felected from the Engliſh, and had educated for clergymen,— was Abbot of Melrofe. He was willing to conform, and was appointed to fucceed Colman as Biſhop of Lindisfarn. The Abbey of Melrofe thus fell under Roman rule, but it continued a simple structure so long as it remained a part of the kingdom of Northumberland. In 1020 the boundaries of Scotland were stretched from the Tweed to the Cheviots, and the part of Northumberland now called Roxburghshire became part and parcel of Scotland. In course of time the establishment at Melrose declined, the house became ruinous, and the abbey was granted to the monks of Coldingham during those religious times when the monks had much to ask, and the king and barons much to give. A hamlet, now called Old Melrose, still marks the site of the ancient house.

In 1136 the pious David raised a new and much superior abbey, about two miles westward of the original site, but on the same south bank of the Tweed, and established in it the Cistercians. He conferred on them extensive lands and privileges; the lands of Melros, Eldun, and Dernwie; the lands and wood of Gattonside, with the fishings of the Tweed along the whole extent of those lands; with the right of pasturage and pannage in his forests of Selkirk and Traguair, and in the forest between the Gala and the Leeder, with wood from those forests for building and burning. In 1192 Jocelin, Bishop of Glasgow, granted to the monks of Melrose the church of Hassindean, with its lands, tithes, and other emoluments, "ad susceptionum pauperum et peregrinorum ad donum de Melros venientem." From this cause the old tower of Hassindean was called "Monks' Tower," and the farm adjoining the church is still called "Monks' Croft." In fact, the Abbey of Melrose was a sort of inn, not only to the poor, but to some of the greatest men of the time. The Scottish kings from time to time, and wealthy subjects too, added fresh grants; so that in the twelfth and thirteenth centuries they had accumulated vast possessions and immunities; had many tenants, great husbandmen, with many granges and numerous herds. They had much other property in Ayrſhire, Dumfries-ſhire, Selkirkſhire, and Berwickſhire.

But the abbey church which David built was not that of which we have now the remains. The whole place was repeatedly burnt down by the Engliſh invaders. In 1215 the rebellious barons of King John of England ſwore fealty to Alexander II. of Scotland, at the altar of Melroſe. Edward I., in 1295-6, when at Berwick, granted the monks of Melroſe reſtitution of the lands of which they had been deprived; but in 1322 Edward II. burnt down the abbey and killed the abbot William de Peeblis, and ſeveral of his monks. Robert I., of Scotland, in 1326, or four years afterwards, gave £2,000, ſterling to rebuild it; and Edward III., of England, came from Newcaſtle at Chriſtmas, 1341, and held his yule in the abbey, and made reſtitution of the lands and other property which his father had ſeized during the late war. In 1378 Richard II. granted a protection to the abbot and his lands, but in 1385 he burnt down Melroſe and other religious houſes on his expedition into Scotland. Robert Bruce, in the beginning of the fourteenth century, granted a revenue to reſtore the abbey, and betwixt this period and the Reformation aroſe the ſplendid ſtructure, the ruins of which yet charm every eye. It is in the higheſt ſtyle of the Decorated order, every portion is full of work of the moſt exquiſite character, occaſionally mingled with the Perpendicular. They are only the ruins of the church which remain, and they preſent the fineſt ſpecimen of Gothic architecture and ſculpture that Scotland poſſeſſes. One of Scotland's moſt diſcriminating writers ſays, "To ſay that Melroſe is beautiful, is to ſay nothing. It is exquiſitely—ſplendidly lovely. It is an object poſſeſſed of infinite grace and unmeaſurable charm; it is fine in its general aſpect, and in its minuteſt details. It is a ſtudy—a glory." The church is two

186   MELROSE ABBEY.

hundred and eighty-feven feet in length, and at the greateft
breadth one hundred and fifty-feven feet. The weft is wholly
ruined; but the great eaftern window remains, and one above
the fouthern door, which are extremely fine. The pillars that yet
remain to fupport the roof are of fingular grace, and wherever
you turn you behold objects that rivet the attention by their

MELROSE : THE NAVE.

richnefs of fculpture, though often only in fragments. The
only wonder is that fo much has efcaped the numberlefs
affaults of enemies. During the reigns of Henry VIII.,
Edward VI., and Elizabeth, the abbey was continually fuffer-
ing from their inroads, in which the fpirit of vengeance againft

the Scots who refifted their fchemes of aggreffion was mixed ftrongly with that of enmity to popery. In the year 1545, it was twice burnt and ranfacked by the Englifh, firft under Sir Ralph Eyre and Sir Bryan Layton, and again by the Earl of Hertford. At the Reformation, when all its lands and immunities were invefted in the Crown, they were valued at £1,758 Scots, befides large contributions in kind. Amongft them, in addition to much corn, was one hundred and five ftones of butter, ten dozens of capons, twenty-fix dozens of poultry, three hundred and feventy-fix moor-fowl, three hundred and forty loads of peats, etc. Queen Mary granted Melrofe and its lands and tithes to Bothwell, but they were forfeited on his attainder. They then paffed to a Douglas, and afterwards to Sir James Ramfay, who refcued James VI. in the confpiracy of Gowrie; then to Sir Thomas Hamilton in 1619, who was made Earl of Melrofe, and afterwards Earl of Haddington. About a century ago they became the property of the family of Buccleuch, in which they remain. The Douglas built himfelf a houfe out of the ruins which may ftill be feen about fifty yards to the north of the church. The ruins are preferved with great care, and are fhown by a family which is at once intelligent and courteous. The perfon going round moft generally, points out the fhattered remains of thirteen figures at the great eaftern window, in their niches, faid to have been thofe of our Saviour and his Apoftles. They were broken to pieces by a fanatic weaver of Gattonfide. A head is alfo pointed out, faid to be that of Michael Scott, the magician, who exerted his power fo wonderfully, according to tradition, in this neighbourhood, as to fplit the Eildon Hill into three parts.

Much as they have been hackneyed, we cannot omit the

lines of Scott, on Melrose, from his " Lay of the Last Minstrel," as they are so especially descriptive :—

> If thou wouldst view fair Melrose aright,
> Go visit it in the pale moonlight;
> For the gay beams of lightsome day
> Gild but to flout the ruins gray.
> When the broken arches are dark in night,
> And each shafted oriel glimmers white;
> When the cold light's uncertain shower
> Streams on the ruined central tower;
> When buttress and buttress alternately
> Seem framed in ebon and ivory;
> When silver edges the imagery,
> And the scrolls that teach thee to live and die;
> When distant Tweed is heard to rave,
> And the owlet to hoot o'er the dead man's grave.
> Then go—but go alone the while—
> Then view St. David's ruined pile;
> And home returning, soothly swear,
> Was never scene so sad and fair.
>
> . . . .
>
> By a steel-clenched postern door,
>   They entered now the chancel tall;
> The darkened roof rose high aloof
>   On pillars lofty, light and small;
> The key-stone that locked each ribbéd aisle,
> Was a fleur-de-lys, or a quartre-feuille;
> The corbels were carved grotesque and grim,
> And the pillars with clustered shafts so trim,
> With base and capital furnished around,
> Seemed bundles of lances with garlands bound.
>
> . . . .
>
> The moon on the east oriel shone,
> Through slender shafts of shapely stone,
>   By foliaged tracery combined :
> Then wouldst thou have thought some fairy's hand
> 'Twixt poplars straight the osier wand
>   In many a freakish knot had twined;
> Then framed a spell, when the work was done,
> And changed the willow wreaths to stone.

The name of Melrofe is clearly derived from the Ancient Britifh, Mellrofs, the *projection of the meadow*. Moel in Welfh and Maol in Irifh fignify fomething bald, naked, bare. Thus Maol-Rofs, in the language of the Irifh monks who firft built a church here, would fignify the naked promontory. Moel in Welfh is now ufually applied to a fmooth mountain, as Moel-Siabod: and we find Rofs continually fhowing its Celtic origin where there is a promontory, as Rofs on the Moray-frith, and Rofs in Herefordfhire from a winding of the Wye. But fome old fculptor, on a ftone ftill preferved in the village, has made a punning derivation for it, by carving a *mell*, or mallet, and a rofe over it. This ftone was part of a wall of the old prifon, long fince pulled down.

The fite of Melrofe, like all monaftic ones, is fine. The abbey ftands on a broad level near the Tweed, but is furrounded by hills and fields full of beauty, and peopled with a thoufand beings of romance, tradition, and poetry. South of the village rife the three peaks of the Eildon hill, bearing aloft the fame of Michael Scott and Thomas the Rhymer. On the banks of the Tweed, oppofite to Melrofe, lies Gattonfide, buried in its gardens and orchards, and ftill retaining its faith in many a ftory of the fuper-natural; and about three miles weftward, on the fame bank of the river, ftands Abbotsford, raifed by a magician more mighty than Michael Scott. How is it poffible to approach that haunted abode without meeting on the way the moft wonderful troop of wild and lofty and beautiful beings, that ever peopled earth or the realm of imagination? Scotch, Englifh, Gallic, Indian, Syrian come forth to meet you. The Bruce, the Scottifh Jamefes, Cœur de Lion, Elizabeth, Leicefter, Mary of Scots, James I. of England, Montrofe, Claverhoufe, Cumberland the Butcher. The Covenanters are ready to preach and fight anew, the Highland clans rife in aid of the Stuart. What women of dazzling beauty—Flora M'Ivor, Rofe Bradwardine, Rebecca the noble Jewefs, Lucy Afhton, and Amy Robfart, the lovely Effie Deans, and her homely yet glorious fifter Jenny, the bewitching Die Vernon, and Minna and Brenda Troil, of the northern ifles, ftand radiant amid a hoft of leffer beauties. Then comes Rob Roy, the Robin Hood of the hills; then Balfour of Burley iffues, a ftalwart apparition, from his hiding-places, and of infinite humour and ftrangenefs of afpect. Where is there a band like this—the Baron of Bradwardine, Dominie Sampfon, Meg Merrilies, Monkbarns, Edie Ochiltree, Old Mortality, Bailie Nicol Jarvie, Andrew Fairfervice, Caleb Balderftone, Flibbertigibbet, Norna of the Fitful Head, and that fine fellow the farmer of Liddesdale, with all his Peppers and Muftards yaffling at his heels? But not even out of Melrofe need you move a ftep to find the name of a faithful fervant of Sir Walter. Tom Purdie lies in Melrofe Abbey-yard, and Scott himfelf had engraven on his tomb that he was "the Wood-forefter of Abbotsford," probably the title which Tom gave himfelf. Thofe who vifit Melrofe will like to take a peep at the graveftone of Tom Purdie, who fleeps amid a long line of the dead, reaching from the days of Aidan to our own, as alive he filled a little niche in the regards of a mafter who has given to both high and low fo many niches in the temple of immortality.

ABBOTSFORD.

The calm of evening o'er the dark pine wood,
Lay with an aureate glow as we explored
Thy claffic precincts, hallowed Abbotsford !
And at thy porch in admiration ftood :

We felt thou wert the work, the abode of him
Whofe fame had fhed a luftre on our age;
The mightieft of the mighty, o'er whofe page
Thoufands fhall hang until Time's eye grow dim;—
And then we thought, when fhall have paffed away
The millions now purfuing life's career,
And Scott himfelf is duft,—how, lingering here,
Pilgrims from all the lands of earth fhall ftray
Amid thy maffive ruins, and furvey,
The fcenes around with reverential fear!
       DAVID MACBETH MOIR.

Carisbrooke Castle.

ABOUT a mile weſt of Newport, the remains of this ancient caſtle ſtand on a ſteep, circular, and apparently artificial hill. This knoll was probably raiſed by the ancient Britiſh on the ſummit of a range of chalk hills, which command an extenſive view. No remains of thoſe early times appear to exiſt. The keep at the north-eaſt angle ſtanding on a mound conſiderably higher than the other buildings, and which is of a multangular form, has been aſcribed to the Saxons, who had a caſtle here, but probably it only ſtands on the ſite of the Saxon keep. In the ſixth century it is ſtated to have been a place of great ſtrength, and to have had a well in the interior no leſs than three hundred and ten feet deep, which has ſince been filled up, there being another in the caſtle-yard of nearly the ſame depth. The old caſtle covered leſs than two acres of ground, but, from ſucceſſive additions, eſpecially in the reign of Elizabeth, its remains cover about twenty acres.

The approach to the caſtle is by a gateway leading to a ſecond. The ſmaller external gate was built by Queen Elizabeth: her initials and the date, 1598, appearing upon it. With the exception of this gate, the additions of Elizabeth appear to have been confined to the outer wall, which ſhe enlarged ſo as to comprehend its preſent extent; and to the domeſtic buildings, none of which appear older than her time. Amongſt theſe

CARISBROOKE; GATEWAY.

latter are fhown part of the chapel in which Charles I. was confined, with the window through which he attempted to efcape.

The moft modern building of the whole is the chapel of St. Nicholas, rebuilt on the fite of a more ancient one, by George II., in 1738. In this chapel the mayor of Newport and the high conftables are ftill fworn into office, either by the governor of the ifland or his deputy.

Advancing through the firft and fmaller gate, you behold the fecond and much grander one, flanked by two noble round towers. This was probably built by Lord Woodville, in the reign of Edward IV., for his arms are yet vifible upon it. This afpect of the caftle is extremely picturefque. The gateway is ftrikingly impreffive, and the mouldering battlements, hung with luxuriant ivy, give to it the folemnity of ruin. At the fouth-eaft angle of the caftle is an ancient tower, called Montjoy's, the walls of which are in fome places eighteen inches thick. But no part of the ancient remains is fuppofed to be of a higher date than the Norman period, erected by William Fitz-Ofborne, its firft Norman lord, and his immediate fucceffors. Confiderable additions were made in the reign of Henry I.

The buildings erected for the accommodation of the governor of the ifland, when he chooses or has occafion to refide here, are extenfive, but by no means magnificent; nor particularly cheerful, having only one window which looks out beyond the enclofure of the caftle, or gives any view of the extenfive but fomewhat naked landfcape which the caftle commands. In fact, one of the moft ftriking features of the Ifle of Wight at the prefent day is its abfence of wood. It is girdled by woodlands round its coafts, but its interior is one monotonous fcene of undulating and neatly cultivated land—a land almoft without a tree. The name of Carifbrooke has been varioufly derived from Whitgara-burgh, the town of Whitgara, a Saxon chief, and from Caer, the old Britifh name for a ftronghold, and brook, referring to the brook in the valley below. Neither of thefe appear to us very fatisfactory. More probably the Whitgara was but a corruption of Hvitgård, the Scandinavian for white refidence; and Carifbrooke comes from the Saxons having added their burg to the Britifh caer, though meaning the fame thing, a caftle or fort; and the burg, as in Germany, being gradually corrupted into bruck, as in Ofnabruck, Innfbruck; and fo to brooke, Caerfbruck, and thence to Carifbrooke.

The well in the caftle-yard is, with much probability, ascribed to the Romans. They are known to have had poffeffion of the ifland in the reign of the emperor Claudius; and the work is like one of their bold undertakings. The water is drawn up by means of a large wheel, within which an afs treads, and thus produces a rotatory motion. It is, in fact, an afinine treadmill. Yet thefe animals feem to enjoy a wonderful longevity in their Gibeonite office. They are always fet to work to fetch up water for the amufement of vifitors; a lighted candle or lamp being alfo let down to fhow the immenfe depth. Formerly the vifitors ufed to drop pins down; but this is now properly prohibited, as likely to injure the quality of the water. One of the affes, we are told, performed the office of turning the wheel for *forty-five* years, and another for *twenty-eight*.

The inhabitants of the neighbouring town of Newport appear to be allowed by the governor of Carifbrooke Caftle to celebrate fome of their focial feftivities in the hall there. At a late vifit by a friend of ours, women were fcrubbing the floor, and perfons putting up flags, in preparation for the annual banquet of an Odd Fellows' Lodge: whilft at the fame time tents were erected within the ruins, and the gaieties of a flower-fhow were proceeding.

In the grounds of the neighbouring vicarage, in 1859, the foundations of a Roman villa were difcovered, with a beautiful teffellated pavement, which are now fhown. In the neighbourhood are alfo veftiges of an ancient priory. Carifbrooke has the reputation of being the only ancient fortrefs ever erected in the ifland.

But the circumftance which gives its chief intereft to the caftle is the fact of the confinement of Charles I. there by the Parliament, from November 1647, to September of the following year. The circumstances which led him thither have occasioned, perhaps, as much controversy as any historical event of that troubled age. Clarendon—who is supposed not to have liked John Ashburnham, who principally induced Charles to seek refuge in the Isle of Wight, because he was more in the confidence of the king than himself—has given an account of the flight of the king, which, though confused and inconsistent in itself, seems nearly, if not entirely, to accuse Ashburnham and Berkeley, who accompanied Charles with Major Legg, of treason to their master. Both Ashburnham and Berkeley have written narratives of the transaction, and Clarendon states distinctly that he had carefully read and considered those narratives before he composed his "History of the Rebellion," and yet he makes various statements unwarranted by either.

Charles was at Hampton Court, and the Parliamentary army was encamped on Putney Heath. He was under the surveillance of the army: and had been in active correspondence with the leading officers of it, endeavouring to come to terms of agreement for his restoration. Cromwell and his son-in-law, Ireton, appeared at that time quite earnestly to desire his restoration: and conditions were submitted to Charles by what were termed the adjutators, or "agitators," of the army. The king could not bring himself to accept them. Jealousies sprang up amongst the officers; some of them thinking Cromwell and Ireton too much disposed to allow Charles to recover the crown on terms advantageous to themselves and dangerous to the rest. The levelling part of the adjutators declared, or were said to declare, that they would seize on Charles, and, if he did not accord with their desires, would kill him. Such were the circumstances when Charles suddenly escaped in the night with Sir John Berkeley, Mr. John Ashburnham, and Mr. William Legg, gentlemen in attendance on him, but who had lately been removed by order of the parliament. They accompanied him to Tichfield, a feat of the Earl of Southampton, and Afhburnham and Berkeley were fent thence to feek an interview with Colonel Hammond, the governor of the Ifle of Wight, which ended in Charles's reception by the governor, and his fubfequent imprifonment and delivery to the parliament.

Clarendon fays that there is no clear ftatement in the narratives of his two attendants " of any probable inducement to prevail with the king to undertake the journey," and that he had fought in thefe narratives, in vain, what the motives might be which led to fo fatal a refult.—" That when they fet off the king had certainly no intention of going to the Ifle of Wight."—That on the road he afked Afhburnham " where the fhip was ?" And he blames this gentleman extremely for not having procured a fhip after having engaged to do fo. All thefe are very ftrange affertions, as every one who examines thofe narratives muft perceive. The motives which led Charles to think of the Ifle of Wight are all clearly detailed by Afhburnham : no fhip is mentioned in Berkeley's relation, except that the king faid he had heard that *he* had one at Portsmouth; to which Sir John replied that the whole was a fable and an impoffibility, becaufe he had not a penny to procure one with. In Afhburnham's narrative, he himfelf gives as a reafon for Charles's concealment in the Ifle of Wight, that, as he was in treaty with the Scots, it would be fatal to leave England altogether, and that, if he defired it, it would require fome time to procure a fhip. No queftion on the journey was afked by Charles, of Afhburnham, " Where is the fhip?" becaufe he knew very well from Berkeley that there was none. The whole fcheme of the flight had been duly difcuffed, and was underftood by the whole party before fetting out. Yet on fuch grounds does Clarendon fay,

"He not being sure of a ship, if the resolution were fixed for embarking, which was never manifest—the making choice of the Isle of Wight, and of Hammond to be trusted, since nothing fell out which was not reasonably to be foreseen and expected—and the bringing him to Tichfield, without the permission of the king, if not directly contrary to it—seemed to be all so far from a rational design and conduct, that most men did believe that there was treason in the contrivance," etc.

Now, the whole story is very simple and clear in the narratives of these gentlemen; and, with the exception of letting Hammond know that Charles was near, and allowing him to go with them to him, which was very foolish, is far from any blame on their part. The fact was, as stated, that Charles was afraid of his person being seized by the adjutators, and therefore determined to get away. But, as he was in treaty with the Scots, he distinctly declared that he would not leave England altogether. Under these circumstances, Ashburnham, who was greatly trusted by Charles, and acted as his treasurer, recommended that he should seek concealment at the house of Sir John Oglander, in the Isle of Wight. He might then learn how Colonel Hammond, the governor, was affected towards him, who had lately professed himself extremely well affected, and, in the meantime, he would be out of the way of the adjutators. The king freely accepted this scheme: and at nine o'clock on the evening of the 10th of November, he being supposed to be gone to bed, slipped out; and Legg, Ashburnham, and Berkeley, received him at a postern-door in the garden at Hampton Court, where they all mounted and rode away. They went first to Oatlands through the forest, got lost in the dark, came to Sutton, where a servant was waiting for them, and, finding a Parliamentary committee sitting in the house, did not go in to breakfast, but rode on towards Southampton. On the way Charles said he would not go direct to the island, but would stop at Tichfield—the house of the Earl of Southampton, where the Earl's mother was staying—whilst Ashburnham and Berkeley went over and sounded the governor. This was done; and here occurs the only discrepancy of any moment in the accounts of the narrators. Ashburnham says that Berkeley weakly let it out that the king was not far off, and was coming to the island to throw himself on the protection of the governor; and Berkeley says that it was Ashburnham who did this. Unfortunately it was done, and Hammond, who was a great friend of Cromwell's, was thrown into violent agitation at the predicament into which he was thrown between his regard for the king and his honour as the officer of the parliament. But he pledged himself to deserve the king's confidence, as a man of honour and honesty. He entreated that he might accompany them to bring in the king; and, though they at first objected, they were again weak enough to comply. When they arrived at Tichfield, accompanied also by Basket, governor of Cowes, and Ashburnham went up to the king, and told him what they had done, Charles exclaimed that they had undone him, and that he felt convinced that, in spite of what the governor had pledged, he would make him a prisoner. Ashburnham replied, that this should not be the case: if the king declined to go, they were strong enough, and he would soon dispose of the governor and his companion, the governor of Cowes. But this disposing of by dispatching—which was what Ashburnham meant—Charles would not consent to. He took a fresh pledge from Hammond, and went with him.

The upshot was certain. No sooner did the parliament learn where the fugitive monarch was, than they ordered Hammond to keep him fast: and he did so. Charles's three attendants were dismissed, and a strict guard was kept over him. But his three faithful followers did not desert him. They contrived to correspond with him, and a plan was laid for his escape to France to join the queen. He wrote a letter to Henrietta, desiring her to send a vessel for him, which was done. The vessel lay at Southampton as a merchant vessel with French commodities for sale. But the winds proved contrary, and before they changed, Charles was not allowed to ride out as he had been, but was confined to the walls of the castle. It was then agreed that he should at night escape out of his window, and horses were in secret waiting to convey him to Osborne, and so to Cowes, and over to Southampton to the queen's ship. Charles had found that he could pass his head through the window, and he thence concluded from a popular saw that where the head could pass the body could follow. But in this, as in all his affairs, poor Charles had put his head through the wrong way, that is, with the face foremost, and not sideways, in which the head being longer is the test. He had for years been trying to draw his body through the British constitution, because he thought he had got his head through it; yet he had signally failed. And so it proved in this case: he had to send word the next morning to his friends, that, though he had got his head through, he could not get his body through, and after much straining had got back again, though he had for some time stuck quite fast.

The attempt got wind. In fact, Cromwell wrote to Hammond that the committee at Derby House had full information regarding it; and accordingly, not only was the king more strictly watched, but his three followers, now Ashburnham, Legg, and Levett, were seized and conveyed separately to Arundel, Warwick, and Wallingford castles. After a time, Ashburnham was liberated, and ordered to keep himself at his own house in Sussex, and not to go nearer to London. Notwithstanding, he still maintained a correspondence with Charles, and engaged in other schemes to effect his escape once again from the Ifle of Wight, and once from St. James's in London. He was called upon to compound for his own liberty by the facrifice of half his eftate, and was purfued by inceffant actions for £40,000, for which he had made himfelf refponfible to different creditors whilft private treafurer to the king. As for the king himfelf, hiftory has made us all familiar with his

CARISBROOKE CASTLE.

melancholy ftory. His enemies found a wider window for him at Whitehall than he found for himfelf at Carifbrooke, through which he efcaped from them into the great liberty of the invifible.

After Charles's death, Carifbrooke was made the place of

2 D

detention of his children, and there is a touching ſtory of one of them connected with the place.

After the death of Charles I., Cariſbrooke became the place of confinement of two of his children, Henry, Duke of Glouceſter, and the princeſs Elizabeth. Charles and James were on the continent, as well as the infant princeſs Henrietta, who was with her mother in Paris. As if to add to the unhappineſs of theſe children, they were on the execution of their father removed from London to Cariſbrooke, the ſcene of his former impriſonment. Elizabeth was about thirteen years of age, Henry about eight. The parliament had talked of putting Elizabeth apprentice to a button-maker, and Henry to a ſhoe-maker. Henry was not of an age to feel much their ſituation; but Elizabeth is deſcribed by Père Gamache as a princeſs of a high and courageous ſpirit, poſſeſſing a proud conſciouſneſs of the grandeur of her birth and deſcent. Meditating in her ſolitude on the calamities of her father, and the fall of her houſe, ſhe ſank into a ſlow and fatal fever. When ſhe found herſelf ill, ſhe refuſed to take medicine. She expired alone, ſitting in her apartments at Cariſbrooke, her fair cheek reſting on the Bible, the laſt gift of her father, and which had been her only conſolation during the concluding months of her life. She died on the eighth of September, 1650, in her fifteenth year: and was obſcurely buried at Newport on the twenty-fourth of the ſame month. "All the royal family," ſays Père Gamache, "conſidering her great talents and charms of perſon, had reckoned on her as a means of forming ſome high alliance, which would better their fortunes."

Rievaux Abbey.

IN the old "Magna Britannia" the origin of the founding of this famous abbey is thus quaintly given. "A monaſtery of Ciſtercian monks was built at Rievaux by Walter Eſpec, a great man in the court of Henry I., upon this occaſion. In his youth he had married a certain lady, named Adeline, and had by her a ſon, named Walter, a comely perſon, and the joy of his heart. This his ſon took much delight in ſwift horſes, which at a time ſpurring to run paſt his ſtrength, occaſioned him to ſtumble and fall, whereby he broke his neck, to the great grief of his famous father. By this misfortune Walter, the father, who had acquired a great eſtate by his ſeveral public employments,—namely, a general in war and a juſtice itinerant in peace,—was deprived of an heir, and was at ſome loſs how to diſpoſe of it, till by conſultation with his uncle, William Eſpec, then rector of Garton, he was adviſed to make Chriſt his heir of part of it at leaſt; as he accordingly did, by building and endowing a monaſtery here, at Kirkham, as is before obſerved, and at Waxdon, in Bedfordſhire. The reſt of his eſtates he left to his three ſiſters, of whom Adeline, who married Peter de Ros, had the patronage of this houſe. This priory was furniſhed with monks at firſt ſent by St. Bernard, Abbot of Clarevallis."

Dugdale ſays that Walter Eſpec became a monk in his own

priory, and was buried in it in 1153. So alfo Peter de Ros, who married his fifter Adeline. Many were the benefactors to this monaftery, and it received large eftates and privileges. At the diffolution, Richard Blyton, lord abbot, and twenty-three monks, furrendered the foundation to the commiffioners of Henry VIII., and had a hundred marks affigned him, per annum, for his life. The net refources of the houfe were valued at £278 10s. 2d.

"Aelred, who was abbot in 1140," fays Dugdale, "was an, if not the only, eminent perfon in his houfe for piety, learning, and all the virtues of a monaftic life:" which is not faying much for the piety and learning of Rievaux. Aelred, we are told, became fo famous for his abilities and good qualities, that David, king of Scotland, invited him to go there, but he refufed all worldly honours, refufed even to be made a bifhop, and gave himfelf up to contemplation and preaching. "He imitated St. Bernard in all his actions, being mild, modeft, humble, pious, chafte and temperate, and wonderfully for peace." Yet he muft have been tolerably induftrious, for " he hath written many books of hiftory, piety, and divinity, namely: The Lives of King Edward the Confeffor, and fome other kings of England, in verfe and profe, of David, king, and Margaret, queen of Scotland, and St. Ninian, bifhop; of miracles in general, and of thofe of the Church of St. Hagulftadt in particular, with the ftate of the fame; Chronicles from Aidan; and the Wars of the Standard; of the foundation of St. Margaret's of York, and of Fountains; feveral homilies and fermons."

Yet Dugdale, feeming to recollect himfelf, tells us that Walter Daniel, a monk of this houfe, was his difciple, and equalled him in fome things, and furpaffed him in others. He, too, wrote many things, and on many fubjects, as of the conception and virginity of St. Mary; of true friendſhip; of the burden of the Beaſt of the South; a hundred homilies; and many volumes on the words "HE WAS SENT," etc. All this valuable literature, and much more, we are told, was diſperſed, if not wholly loſt, at the diſſolution.

Walter Eſpec, the founder of Rievaux, is deſcribed as a man of gigantic ſize and of eminent bravery, and as one of the chief commanders in the battle of the Standard. He only lived about two years after retiring to this monaſtery. His gifts to the monks ſeem to have been moſt lordly. His manſion at Kirkham he gave up, and it was converted into a priory. Probably he abandoned this noble manſion becauſe it was near it, on the way to Frithly, that his ſon was killed by his horſe ſtumbling near a ſtone croſs. The eſtates given up there appear to have been large, according to the catalogue of them; and he endowed the priory with ſeven churches and their impropriations, three of them in Northumberland. On the contrary, this abbey of Rievaux, though it had extenſive lands, with paſturage for four thouſand ſheep and cattle, beſides free warren and other privileges, did not poſſeſs one church or chapel beſides the church of the abbey itſelf.

When the abbey was firſt eſtabliſhed in the twelfth century, the country all around it was a wild wildernefs of almoſt unbroken woods, abounding with animals, but with very few men. One William came there with his little company of monks, and ſet about at once to erect a monaſtery, which probably was ſmall and rude. Theſe monks were of the Ciſtercian order, and the abbey, like all their houſes, was dedicated to the Virgin Mary. The habit of this order was a white robe of the nature of a caſſock, with a black ſcapular and a hood, and they had a girdle of woollen cord. In the choir they had a white cowl, and over it a hood, with a rochet hanging down before to the waift, and in a point behind to the calf of the leg; and when they went abroad they wore a cowl and a hood, all black, which was alfo the choir habit. Their difcipline was extremely fevere, abounding in vigils day and night.

Any one ftanding on the fine terrace called Duncombe-terrace, which looks down upon the abbey, may form an idea of the almoft frightful folitude and favagenefs of the place in the early days of the eftablifhment. Grainge, in his "Caftles and Abbeys of Yorkfhire," fays:—" The ruins of the abbey are fituate in a deep, narrow valley, near the Rye, a rapid mountain-ftream flowing from the picturefque valley of Bilsdale, and the bleak moors of Snilefworth. In the immediate neighbourhood of the ruins, half a dozen lateral valleys open out their fides, and pour their babbling brooks into the Rye, thus prefenting great variety of fcenery; and fuch are the windings of the main valley, that, looking from the abbey, it appears on all fides furrounded by hills clothed in wood, rifing to the level of the moors above; the central point of a magnificent natural amphitheatre: a grand framework of natural beauty enclofing a noble relic of ancient art."

But imagine this fcene, not as now, when feven hundred years of cultivation have paffed over it, but when enveloped in denfe woods, this network of winding valleys choked with tangled brufhwood and briars, with no cottage-fmoke to cheer the dark glades, no little crofts or farms to break its monotony, and no voice but of the leaping waters refounding through its pathlefs glens. What a dreary hufh! What a gloomy mantle of brooding obfcurity muft have lain on this hidden ifolated houfe of perpetual faftings, watchings, and penances! We are told that in thofe days the only way to the abbey was by a fingle path, which wound here and there amid the labyrinth of tangled wood. One of its brethren grew weary of this monotony of life—of the ſtrictneſs of Ciſtercian diſcipline—of the vaſt and deſert ſtillneſs that lay like a nightmare on the place, and reſolved to make his eſcape. He plunged into the woods and hurried deſperately along, threading the thickets, wading through moraſſes, clambering up rugged ſteeps, but becoming only the more involved in the intricacies of theſe dales and foreſts. Still he hoped eventually to reach ſome habitable ſpot ; and towards ſunſet, juſt as the ſhadows caſt a deeper gloom, his wiſh was accompliſhed. He caught the ſound of a bell, and hurried wildly towards it. Soon above the trees peered the towers and ſpires of a lordly building. He drew near and gazed in amazement—not on the hoſpitable caſtle of ſome neighbouring baron, but on the carved and crocketed front of his own abbey, which he had left in the morning.

The poor monk had experienced what many a wanderer in unknown wilds has experienced, both before and ſince—what the Auſtralian terms being "buſhed." Confounded by the blinding denſeneſs of the foreſt, thrown from his intended track by unexpected obſtacles, he had grown anxious, and from his anxiety confuſed. In ſuch a condition all idea of the quarters of the heavens are loſt, and the alarmed wanderer goes round in a circuit when he imagines that he is going directly onwards. Many a man in the vaſt woods of new regions has thus gyrated from day to day till he has fallen exhauſted, and left his bones to ſtartle in after years ſome perhaps equally bewildered traveller. The monk of Rievaux, more fortunate, on recognizing his old abode, ſaid " The hand of God is in it !" deſcended the hill, rang the bell, and begged to be again admitted amongſt the brethren.

In the courſe of time Rievaux, or the abbey in the vale of Rye, became the head of the Ciſtercian order in England. At the feaſt given by Nevill, archbiſhop of York, on his inſtallation in 1464, the abbot of Rievaux ranked fourth in the order of precedence at table. The abbey flouriſhed for more than four hundred years, and was preſided over by thirty-three abbots, of whom Aelred, the hiſtorian of the " Battle of the Standard," was the third. As ſtated, it was ſurrendered to the commisſioners of Bluff Harry, by Richard de Blyton ; its groſs income being at that time upwards of £300 per annum, and its net as ſtated above. The plate of the church amounted to five hundred and ſixteen ounces. Some of the tombs, as well as the altar, were richly adorned: that of the abbot Aelred being liberally ornamented with gold and ſilver. A hundred fodder of lead was ſtripped from its roofs by the commiſſioners, its fine bells carried away, and it was left in its then auguſt ſplendour to the inſults and ravages of the long-reſtrained elements. Its ſite was granted by Henry, in exchange for other lands, to Thomas Lord Roſs, Earl of Rutland, a deſcendant of the Eſpec family, through Peter de Ros, who married one of the ſiſters of the great Walter. Peter de Ros, and others of his family, both knights and ladies, were buried here, and others at the priory of Kirkham. The property deſcended by marriage to the Duke of Buckingham, and in 1695 it was ſold by George, the ſecond duke, to Sir Charles Duncombe, an anceſtor of Lord Feverſham, the preſent owner. This George, Duke of Buckingham, was that George Villiers ſo notorious for his profligacy, and whoſe miſerable end, in a ſmall inn at Kirby Moorſide, Pope has ſo graphically deſcribed :—

> In the worſt inn's worſt room, with mat half-hung,
> The floors of plaſter, and the walls of dung ;
> On once a flock-bed, but repair'd with ſtraw,
> The tape-tied curtains never meant to draw :
> The George and Garter dangling from that bed,
> Where tawdry yellow ſtrove with dirty red,

> Great Villiers lies*—alas! how changed from him,
> That life of pleasure, and that foul of whim!
> Gallant and gay, in Clevedon's proud alcove,
> The bower of wanton Shrewsbury,† and love,
> Or just as gay, at council, in a ring
> Of mimick'd statesmen, and their merry king.
> No wit to flatter, left of all his store;
> No fool to laugh at, which he valued more.
> There, victor of his health, of fortune, friends,
> And fame, this lord of useless thousands ends!
> His grace's fate sage Cutler‡ could foresee,
> And well (he thought) advised him, " Live like me."
> As well his grace replied, " Like you, Sir John?
> That I can do, when all I have is gone!"
> Resolve me, Reason, which of these is worse,
> Want with a full or with an empty purse?
> Thy life more wretched, Cutler, was confess'd,
> Arise, and tell me, was thy death more bless'd?"
>
> POPE'S MORAL ESSAYS.

The stranger, in visiting Rievaux, should take his first view of it from what is called the Duncombe-terrace. Proceeding along a winding carriage-drive, you are admitted at a lodge-gate, and suddenly find yourself on one of the finest natural terraces imaginable. This is now kept beautifully smooth, and is adorned at each end by Grecian temples, the interiors of which have been enriched with paintings by Bernici. But the most striking scene is without; for you find yourself on the edge of the noble terrace, looking down into a deep valley, out of which rises, like an apparition of the past, the ruined pile of Rievaux. The effect is most impressive. There deep below

---

* This lord, yet more famous for his vices than his misfortunes, after having been possessed of about £50,000 a-year, and passed through many of the highest posts in the kingdom, died in the year 1687 in a remote inn in Yorkshire, reduced to the utmost misery.

† " Shrewsbury."—The Countess of Shrewsbury, a woman abandoned to gallantries. The Earl, her husband, was killed by the Duke of Buckingham in a duel; and it has been said that during the combat she held the Duke's horse in the habit of a page.

‡ " Cutler," a notorious miser.

rises the lofty shattered fabric of this once magnificent abbey, silent as in the hush of ages. Near it a little rustic hamlet, the smoke of whose chimneys ascends with a peacefulness as if still touched by the monastic spirit of the place. Around stretch wooded valleys and ancient pastoral hills, seeming yet lovingly to enshrine this vision of beauty reaching us from the days of a once proud hierarchy, that never dreamed of its temples and cœnobia standing as warnings of the vanity of all ambition, even of that which thinks it has laid eternal foundations in the hopes and fears of the human soul. But let us descend.

The chief remains are those of the transept and the choir, with a portion of the main tower standing at the junction of the transept, and what once was the nave, but of which only the foundation can now be traced. What, in fact, is the present transept, must have been the body of the original church. It bears all the stamp of that early period. Its small, and, for the most part, round-headed windows and rude masonry tell of the Norman period of the days of Walter Espec. The tower is short and broad, like most Norman towers, with its tall narrow lancet windows; but the choir has all the air of a later day. The lofty pillars, its pointed and often deeply-moulded arches, and all its carvings, are of much more advanced style. The whole length of the church was three hundred and forty-eight feet: the nave being one hundred and sixty-six feet long by sixty-three wide; the transept one hundred and eighteen feet long and thirty-three wide. The arch opening from the transept into the choir is seventy-five feet high, and the circumference of the base of each pillar is thirty feet. The side aisles are divided from the centre by eight clustered columns on each side; above is the triforium arcade, consisting of fourteen arches on each side; above which is a passage along both fides of the choir, going paſt the windows. The brackets of the columns, riſing from between the arches of the lower arcade, are adorned with foliage finely carved, yet as freſh as when firſt cut.

Though the *tout enſemble* of the church is broken up by ruin, it yet preſents to the eye of the imagination the noble

RIEVAUX: OLD GATEWAY.

aſpect of the whole when it was complete and in uſe; its windows filled with painted glaſs, and the incenſe floating in clouds amongſt its lofty groins and traceried capitals, and the ſound of anthems ſwelling from the choir. The place is worthy of all its fame. The floors of the choir and tranſept were cleared of their loads of rubbish in 1819, thus leaving the full height and other proportions of these beautiful remains of English art clear. In 1821 a part of a tessellated pavement was laid bare, near the high altar, and in it were wrought the letters Abe Maria gr. This is now preserved in the circular temple at the south end of Duncombe-terrace. Some fragments of stained glass were also found; and it is worthy of remark that stained glass is first mentioned in the North of England, in 1140, as appearing in the windows of Rievaux.

Most of the other buildings of the abbey, as the cloisters, the abbot's house, the refectory, etc., are in a great state of ruin, and many of them hung with heavy masses of ivy, while the floors are buried beneath heaps of the fallen roofs and walls. But what is this which we have here? On the west side of the refectory there is a mountainous heap of iron slag and cinders, showing that an iron-foundry existed here in some long-past age. It is overgrown with grass, and appears to have been unnoticed, amongst the other mounds and inequalities made up of the fallen materials of the buildings, till late years. When we were there this vast heap was being carted away to mend the roads, and seemed as though it would furnish an excellent supply for that purpose for a very long period. Did the monks, amongst their other occupations, avail themselves of the ore in the neighbourhood, and, bearing the general appellation of "lazy monks," thus employ a portion of their time to their own and the public benefit? There is very little doubt that this was the case. The monks in many places were holders of extensive lands, and industrious improvers of it. They were, in fact, the leaders and stimulators of agriculture, as they were the almost inspired architects and the most exquisite sculptors and carvers of their time. It was not alone in their scriptorium that they copied

missals and breviaries in the most exquisite caligraphy, and
embellished them with equally exquisite paintings; it was not
alone in writing histories of saints and kings that they employed
their time; nor in carving beautiful cups and crucifixes for
their altars; nor in working gorgeous copes and chasubles; but
they extended their attention to all the more rude and matter-
of-fact arts and pursuits of ordinary life. They had farms and
mills, and cider-presses, and fisheries with weirs and traps.
Some of them, as Roger Bacon, Bishop Grostête of Lincoln,
Dunstan, and others, dived deep into the mysteries of chemistry,
and other more occult arts, and nothing is better ascertained
than that out of the quiet of a monastery came forth the
thunder of gunpowder. They had, too, these "lazy monks,"
it now appears clearly, their mines and smelting-houses and
bloomeries. Not only does this huge heap of slags and drosses
bear testimony to the fact, but at Ayton Priory, and in the
Forge Valley, near Scarborough, remain the vestiges of those
mining and iron-smelting concerns in which they were cut
short by the summary commissioners of Henry VIII. We
are informed by our friend J. G. Baker, of Thirsk, in Yorkshire, that a rock of from seven to twelve feet thick, running
through a range of hills near Scarborough, which one of these
monastic brotherhoods worked before the dissolution of their
house, is now again being worked, and promises to yield
twenty thousand tons of iron ore to the acre, producing thirty
per cent. of metal, probably the beginning only of one of the
largest iron-producing tracts in the country. Truly these
"lazy monks" had their redeeming qualities! They were not
all, it would appear, "tarred with the same brush." The
monastic system, though not the most natural or wise of institu-
tions, was in fact censurable not so much for its institution as
for its corruption. It was the light of dark and barbarous

times. It afforded peaceful fpots under the fhadow of its fanctity, amid the perpetual turbulence and ravage of war. It preferved in its libraries the learning of the old world—the Bible amongft the reft; and it originated or perfected the chief arts of the new: architecture, fculpture, carving, caligraphy, painting on canvas, wood, vellum, and glafs. Aftrology, the rude parent of aftronomy; alchemy, the equally rude but cunning-looking parent of chemiftry; botany, and the introduction of new plants and fruits, medicine, and metaphyfics—all received a loving welcome in the cells of monks, and won fubftantial advances at their hands. Agriculture was profecuted with great zeal, efpecially by the Ciftercians; and it now appears that we muft add the refearches of mining and the labour of forges to their lift of induftries. Let us remember the energetic as well as the lazy monks; the fcientific as well as the ignorant; the virtuous and enterprifing as well as the fordid and fenfual; the Bernards, the Bacons, the Grofteftes, and many a fhrewd and diligent labourer who has left no name, as well as the fwinifh herd which roufed the ire and gave fuch pungency to the fatire of Chaucer, who lived in the midft of it. Even as we approach the fallen fhrines of this much and juftly abufed race of men, remembering their many beautiful arts and achievements, and the world of once great and wise hearts which beat there, we may, in the words of Lord Byron, fay—

"Stop, for thy tread is on an empire's duft!"

Furness Abbey.

An apparition hung amid the hush
Of the lone vale; whether exhaled from earth
Or dropt from heaven, as yet my beating heart,
That quaked unto the sudden solitude,
Knew not, nor cared to know—a mist—a cloud—
Material shadow—or a spiritual dream!
Slowly and waveringly it seemed to change
Into a hoary edifice, o'erhung
By hoary trees with mouldering boughs as mute
E'en as the mouldering stones—a ghostlike show!
Uncertain in their tremor where to rest,
Like birds disturbed at night, my startled thoughts
Floated around the dim magnificence
Of air-woven roofs, and arches light as air
Spanning the faded sunset, till the Pile,
Still undergoing, as my spirit gazed
Intenslier and intenslier through the gloom,
Strange transformation from the beautiful
To the sublime, breathing alternately
Life-kindling hope and death-foretelling fear,
Majestically settled down at last
Into its own religious character,
A house of prayer and penitence—dedicate
Hundreds of years ago to God, and Her
Who bore the Son of Man! An abbey fair
As ever lifted reverentially
The solemn quiet of its stately roof
Beneath the moon and-stars.
                             Professor Wilson.

N that remarkable promontory in the north-weſt of Lancaſhire, which runs out into the ſea oppoſite to Walney Iſle, and between the river Duddon and the waters of Morecambe Bay, ſtand the ruins of the once princely abbey of Furneſs. This name it derives from the promontory which anciently bore the name of Fuder-neſſe, or the further noſe or promontory, a Scandinavian name, teſtifying, like ſo many of our promontories which bear the name of neſs, to the one-time ſojourn of the Northmen. This promontory or peninſula, now condenſed into Furneſs, is hemmed in by the hills of Cumberland and Weſt-moreland, and the inland portion of it partaking of the hilly and rocky character of thoſe counties, is known as High Furneſs, or Furneſs Fells. In Low Furneſs, or the portion of lower and more fertile land approaching the ſea, and in a deep glen by the way as you proceed from Ulverſtone to the Iſle of Walney, the monks of Furneſs fixed their ſheltered abode. They exerciſed that tact for which monks were ſo famous in the ſelection of their ſite. Whilſt extending their lordſhip over the higher and wilder diſtricts of the peninſula, where they could enjoy all the privileges of free warren and of the chace, collecting the tribute of its mountain-ſtreams in the ſhape of trout, they had ſeated themſelves amid the paſtoral fatneſs of the land. Beſides this, their territory abounded in ſtone and timber for building, and in wealth of minerals, iron and lead, of which we have had occaſion to note that they fully comprehended the value. The valley in which they erected their abbey was named by the Saxons Bekanſgill, or the valley of Nightſhade, from the growth of that beautiful but deadly plant, the Atropa Belladonna, ſtill to be found flou-

riſhing amid its ruins. So ſays John Still, the poetical hiſtorian of the abbey in the reign of Henry VI.—

> "Hæc vallis tenuit olim ſibi nomen ab herba
> Bekan, qua viruit, dulcis nunc, tunc ſed acerba;
> Inde domus nomen, Beckanſgill, claruit ante."

Hence, too, the nightſhade figures largely in the armorial devices of the ancient ſeal of the abbey.

Furneſs was founded in 1127, by monks from the monaſtery of Savigni, who were invited by Stephen, Earl of Bologne, afterwards King Stephen, to whom the lordſhip had been

FURNESS ABBEY.

granted. Thefe monks were of the Ciftercian order, as was fo generally the cafe with thofe who founded the abbeys of the twelfth century. It is noteworthy that, of the ten abbeys and priories which we have introduced into this volume, the whole of them, without our having felected them on that account, feem either to have been founded or refounded in the twelfth century. Three of thefe—Glaftonbury, Iona, and Melrofe—were ancient Britifh churches, taken poffeffion of and refounded by the Roman Catholics. Of thefe, too, no fewer than nine were poffeffed by the Ciftercian order, and, therefore, with one exception, dedicated, according to their wont, to St. Mary: namely :—

    Fountains, founded 1132, dedicated to St. Mary.
    Rievaux, ditto 1131, ditto ditto.
    Tintern, ditto 1131, ditto ditto.
    Melrofe, refounded 1136, ditto ditto.
    Holyrood, founded 11—, ditto ditto.
    Furnefs, ditto 1127, ditto ditto.
    Lanthony, ditto 1108, ditto St. Auguftine.
    Glaftonbury, refounded 12th cent., Mary and Jefus
    Iona, ditto ditto ditto ditto.

The twelfth century was the period of the afcendancy of the Ciftercian order. Of the feventeen chief abbeys and priories of Yorkfhire, thirteen were founded in that century, and of thefe, fix were Ciftercian. Thofe founded earlier were generally Benedictine, and the later Carthufian or Francifcan.

Furnefs, indeed, had a Benedictine origin, Savigni being originally a houfe of that order; but the fourth abbot of Savigni furrendered the houfe and all its dependencies to St. Bernard, the great abbot of Clairvaux, to become Ciftercian; and though Peter of York, the fourth abbot of Furnefs, went to Rome and obtained an order from the Pope to disobey this ceffion, he was, on his return, feized by the monks of Savigni, and compelled to refign his abbey, and remain a monk there, Furnefs continuing Ciftercian. In its early days Furnefs had alfo a ftruggle for precedence with the abbey of Waverley in Surrey, which was alfo Ciftercian, on the ground that Waverley was founded a little pofterior to it. But it was ruled by the pope that Waverley fhould ftand at the head of all the Ciftercian houfes in England; but that Furnefs fhould ftand fecond, and Rievaux third: though fome authors have placed Rievaux firft.

The charter of Stephen conferred on Furnefs immenfe eftates, which endowed it with almoft regal power. In this and fucceeding charters they are defcribed as poffeffing the right of fifhery in Lancafter, Staplethorne, Furnefs Foreft, the Ifle of Walney, and the chace of Walney, the fifhery of Dalton, Winterburne, Fordbotle, Crinelton, Rofe, Berdefley, Newby, Sellefec, etc. The abbot had, alfo, amongft other privileges, fheriff's term, affize of bread and beer, wreck of the fea, wayf and eftray, infangenetheof, and free chace in Dalton, Kyrkeby, Ireleth, Penyngton, Ulverfton, Aldingham, Legh, and Urfewyk in Furnefs. He was free from county fines and amercements, and from county fuits and wapentakes, for himfelf and men in thofe towns; and to have a market, fair, and gallows in Dalton; with full authority to make fummons and attachments by his bailiff in Furnefs. In fhort he had all the power of a fovereign prince over life and death. The ferjeantry or ftewardfhip was of fuch importance that it was ufually held by men of high rank. In the reign of Edward III. we find Sir Robert de Holland holding this office; and in that of Henry VIII. Cardinal Wolfey foliciting it for Stanley, Earl of Derby.

The fize and fplendour of the abbey was in keeping with

this fecular greatnefs; in thefe refpects it was fecond only to Fountains in Yorkfhire. It continued in this full-blown dignity and wealth till the diffolution, when its revenues amounted, according to Speed, to £766 7s. 10d.; but according to Dugdale to £805 16s. 5d., exclufive of the woods, meadows, paftures, and fifheries, retained by the monks in their own hands, and of the fhares of moneys, mills, and faltworks, which belonged to the abbey. The number of the abbots from firft to laft was thirty-eight. The firft abbot was Evan de Abrineis from Savigni; the laft, who furrendered it to the commiffioners of Henry VIII., on the 9th of April, 1537, was Roger Pyle. By a fingular cuftom, however, of this abbey, only ten abbots are recorded in the mortuary or dead book, for when an abbot had prefided ten years he was tranflated or depofed. All fuch abbots as died before the tenth year were not entered in this book; but only fuch as were allowed to be exceptions to the rule of tranflation or depofition, and to continue abbots beyond their decade till their death. Of thefe there were during the whole time only ten. No other abbey of the fame order had this fingular cuftom.

With their large eftates the monks feem to have exercifed a grand hofpitality. Mr. Weft, in his hiftory of the abbey, fays that in the courfe of a difpute betwixt the abbot and the attorney of the duchy of Lancafter, in 1582, fome curious proofs of this came up. One deponent, aged feventy-eight, faid that he had many times feen the tenants refort to the monaftery on tunning days, fometimes with twenty, fometimes with thirty horfes, and had delivered to every of them firkins or barrels of beer, or ale, each containing ten or twelve gallons; and the fame was worth 10d. or 12d. a barrel at that time. A dozen loaves of bread were delivered to every one that had a barrel of ale or beer; which bread and beer, or ale, were delivered weekly; and every dozen loaves was worth 6*d*. Another deponent had known divers children of the tenants and their fervants to have come from the plough, or other work, into the faid abbey, where they had dinner or fupper; and the children of the faid tenants came divers times to the faid abbey, and were fuffered to come to fchool and learning within the faid monaftery. This was confirmed by a third, who faid there was both a grammar fchool and a fong fchool in the monaftery, to which the children of the tenants that paid penfions were free to come and refort; and that he was at the faid fchool. And Richard Banks depofed that the tenants and their families and children did weekly receive charity and devotion, over and above the relief and commodities before rehearfed, to the value of 40*s*. fterling. The abbot and monks did not fubmit to the deprivation of their fplendid eftate and patronage without a ftruggle. They took a diftinguifhed lead in exciting thofe they had fo long maintained to the celebrated Pilgrimage of Grace.

The remains of the abbey bear the character of their early origin. They combine the maffivenefs of the Saxon with the fuperior grace of the Norman architecture. The roof, being ftripped of its lead, foon fell in, and the work of ruin went rapidly on. That of the chapter-houfe being fpared, the roof did not fall till the middle of the eighteenth century. It was vaulted, and formed of twelve ridged arches, fupported by fix pillars in two rows, at fourteen feet diftance from each other. The entrance, or front, to this graceful building is by one of the fineft circular arches, deeply receding and richly ornamented, with a portico on each fide; the whole fupported by maffive fculptured pillars. A very good defcription of Furnefs in its prefent ftate is given by Edward Baines in his "Companion to the Lakes." He fays, "I turned from the high road into a lane fhaded by oaks, running down a narrow valley, or glen, called the Glen of the Deadly Nightfhade : and at the bottom of this glen, under the folemn fhade of majeftic foreft trees, I came upon the ruins of the famous abbey of Furnefs. I beheld it ftanding with a graffy area in front, and enclofed on each fide by noble groves of plane-tree, afh and oak. Though much fhattered, and having loft the central tower, it is ftill extenfive and magnificent. Lofty walls and arches, cluftered columns, and long-drawn aifles, remain; and the fine fymmetry and noble proportions of the arches contraft moft picturefquely with the rents and fiffures of the pile. The former extent of the building may in fome degree be judged of, when I ftate that what remains meafures five hundred feet from north to fouth, and three hundred from eaft to weft."

"The abbey lies in a nook, apparently fo fecluded that it might be deemed the utmoft corner of the earth; but you have only to afcend the hills on either fide, and you look ahead on the wide world, embracing all the extent of fea and land vifible from the fhores of the bay of Morecambe. The college and the fchool-houfe are the moft complete apartments remaining. The former has an arched roof, ftill quite perfect: its tall narrow windows have no arch, but terminate upwards in the fhape of a pediment. The fchool-houfe is equally perfect, but is fmaller and lefs ornamental."

After defcribing the remains of the kitchens and the noble refectories, he fays,—" Paffing through the cloifters, of which only the fkeletons remain, we entered the church under the great central tower, the lofty arches of which are yet ftanding. The eaftern window is of vaft dimenfions, and its ornamental frame was anciently filled with painted glafs, fome of which yet exifts in the church of Bownefs, Windermere. In the wall at the right of the window, are four ftalls with a fretted canopy, where the priefts fate at intervals during the fervice of mafs, and both its rows of pillars are gone. Their bafes, which remain, fhow that the pillars were alternately round and clustered. Four ftatues of admirable workmanfhip,—two of marble, and two of ftone,—are fhown to the vifitor. One is in chain armour; two others are alfo in armour, and the fourth

FURNESS ABBEY; NORTH TRANSEPT.

is a lady. They are in the recumbent pofture, and have lain upon fepulchral monuments. Near the central tower are three chapels, with pavements of ornamental brickwork, and traces of altars. At the weftern end of the church is a winding ftaircafe, ftill perfect, afcending to the top of the building, from whence you have an interefting view of the ruin. The head of Stephen, the founder of the abbey, and that of Maud, his queen, both crowned, are feen on the outfide of the eaftern window."

The liberty and lordfhip of Furnefs remained in the crown from the period of the diffolution till 1662, when Charles II. granted them to Monk, the Duke of Albemarle, and his heirs, for his fervices in fecuring his return to his throne. The property paffed by Monk's granddaughter, to Henry, duke of Buccleuch, in which family it ftill remains. Some of the leafe-holders of Furnefs previous to the grant by Charles, of the name of Prefton, employed the materials of the abbey to conftruct them a manor-houfe on the former fite of the abbot's houfe. Such is the ftory and the *ftatus quo* of venerable Furnefs :

> And though Time
> Has hufhed the choral anthems, and o'erthrown
> The altar, nor the holy crucifix
> Spared, whereon hung outftretched in agony
> Th' Eternal's vifioned arms, 'tis dedicate
> To prayer and penitence ftill. So faid the hufh
> Of earth and heaven unto the fetting fun,
> Speaking, methought, to nightly-wandering man,
> With a profounder warning than the burft
> Of hymns in morn or evening orifons
> Chanted within imagination's ear,
> By fuppliants, whofe duft hath long been mixed
> With that of the hard ftones on which they flept,
> In cells that heard their penitential prayers ;
> The cloifters, where between the hours of prayer
> The brethren walked in whifpering folitude,
> Or fate with bent-down head, each in his niche
> Fixed as ftone image with his rofary
> In pale hands, dropping on each myftic bead
> To Mary Mother mild a contrite tear.
>
> Professor Wilson.

CONCLUSION.

With this sketch we close our present excursions amongst the Castles and Abbeys of England. Whilst recalling for a moment the past glories of these memorials of a vanished condition of human society in these islands, we have felt strongly, not only the fragmental beauty of their remains, but the lessons and the encouragements that they afford us. They stand amid the fair landscapes of England as if meant only to stud them with gems of additional loveliness; but from amongst their ivy-mantled walls, where huge trees strike their roots into their once hallowed or dreaded pavements, and the wild rose and the wall-flower fling their hues and fragrance from traceried windows once gorgeous with emblazoned glass, there come to us whispers of retribution and of the profound purposes of Providence. In no country besides our own, do we meet with such numbers of the graceful skeletons and fractured bones of the once proud forms of papal greatness. We are so accustomed to regard these with the eye of poetry and pictorial effect, that we almost forget at times the stupendous power of which they are the signs, and of the great conflict and victory of which they preserve the remembrance. How little do we now realize the state, and the veneration amounting to terror, with which these superb palaces and temples of a gigantic priesthood were surrounded! With what feelings an ignorant and simple population gazed on their sculptured towers and quaintly-chiselled pinnacles, and at the sound of their matin or their vesper anthems prostrated their souls before an overshadowing dread which drew its triple force from the powers of earth, of heaven, and of hell—which came armed with assumptions more than regal, from the King of kings, and his vicegerent, sitting afar off on some distant throne, around which, in the clouded imaginations of the long-bowed-down multitude, flashed the lights of Deity, and beneath which roared the fires of delegated damna-

2 G

tion. How little do we now realize the meſſages which came from time to time, from that diſtant but all-potent preſence, blaſting, as it were, the monarch on his throne, hurling him down in the duſt at the feet of legate and nuncio, and ſhutting up the doors of church and grave to his banned and ſhuddering people ! How little feel we the amazing ſtrength of thoſe rumours of this repreſentative of Divinity who went forth amid the duſt-covered heads of nobles, along a path paved with the prone faces of the multitude, and with monarchs proud to hold the bridle and the ſtirrup of his ſteed !—How little the deep reverence which like an aura roſe up from the broad lands and wealthy farms, the dark vaſt foreſts alive with deer and wild cattle, from the ſtreams and the mountains that lay around the palaces of theſe ſatraps of that ſpiritual king, and ſet them above the ſteel-clad barons, themſelves ſo haughty and auguſt. We no longer ſee thoſe great eſtates, thoſe gorgeous houſes, raiſed by the miraculous force of arts which they and kings only could command; thoſe Gothic temples, carved and crocketted and pinacled, with their great ſtoried windows blazing with the colours of the rainbow, and with all the ſolemnities of ſacred record. On us the ſculptured majeſty of monarchs and ſaints no longer looks down from the awful fronts and within the gilded ſhrines of thoſe temples. We approach no longer trembling thoſe high altars glittering with heaped jewels and gold, ſpread with reſplendent tapeſtry, as with the colours of the celeſtial realms, lit by tapers emulating the cluſtered columns that bore up the groined and eſcutcheoned roofs, and amid the blaze of ſun-glowing windows dazzling with pageantry of dyes ; amid canopied tombs, carved as in ſnowieſt ivory, of warriors and kings and prelates; amid the ſound of pealing organs, amid the choral thunder of human voices, mingled in dread harmony like the ſound of heaven's own hofts. No longer with the fame palpitating fouls do we behold the great mitred abbot iffue, with his train like a very army, with crozier and crofs and banner borne before him, and with glittering battle-axes following on ftalwart fhoulders, as he went forth to attend as a great temporal and fpiritual peer in Parliament. No longer do we drop with all our kith and kin on our knees, and, as the folemn dignitary flowly paffes by on his plump mule, in caparifon of damafk and gold, receive the bleffing from his extended hands. Thofe hands! which could, to the general belief, open the gates of Paradife, or lock them up at pleafure; open the place of purgatorial or of more confuming fires!

Such was, during the reign of Rome, the living period of thefe houfes, the heavinefs of the weight that lay on the fouls of men. We can talk of it, but we cannot feel it. It is beyond words, beyond the fubtleft force of re-creative imagination. Such an incubus of death can live and ftretch its bloated body and its dragon wings only over generations blind and catalepfed by ignorance. With our light and our intellectual activity, we can no more infpire ourfelves with a fenfe of that worfe than Egyptian bondage, than we can conceive of fome yet untried ftate of being.

But at once the thunderbolt fell. In the pride and confidence of that great fyftem, it fell. As yet no yellow leaf fhone ominous on its tree; as yet no trembling paralyfis of age fhook it, no grey hair drooped on its temple; but in the luftrous day and fummer of its ftrength the thunder crafhed, and the ruins of its glory ftrewed the earth. The irate hand of the temporal ftruck down the fpiritual Titan. The ftout arm of the Tudor, ftrung by paffion and refentment, ftruck, and broke, the livid arm of Rome. Three hundred years have paffed, and the power which was fo wounded lives on elfewhere.

It is only now that the temporal papacy totters to its fall, whilſt its ſpiritual influence ſtill lives, and ſhall long live, over vaſt lands. But here theſe ruins ſtand, as the Jews ſtand amid the Chriſtian world, ſignificant monuments of what has been, and yet ſhall be. They tell us that if any enemy oppreſſes us, if any power in its haughty tyranny lead us to queſtion whether God and Juſtice ſtill live—God and Juſtice do live, and ſalvation will ſurely come in the appointed time. It may not wait till the injury has grown old and feeble; but a ſummer cloud may bring the electric flaſh, and the blue regenerate ſky ſhine out above us, ere we can well have ſaid—" God defend us !"

And now, from theſe fallen haunts and tabernacles of the paſt ſpiritual dynaſty, come up more reconciled and muſical voices. The wrath and the reſentment have died out, and we remember only the beauties and the benefits. We recall the works of literature preſerved, the ſcience delved after, the arts cheriſhed, and the benevolence practiſed towards the poor. We ſeek, though yet with unequal ſucceſs, to revive the architectural genius which evolved theſe fallen fanes; amid their crumbling ſtones and claſping ivy we ſeek for principles of grace and truth; and theſe point us ſmilingly to that inexhauſtible ſource whence mediæval builders drew their laws and forms—to all-informing, God-informed Nature. To theſe voices, to this great ſchoolmiſtreſs, we cannot liſten too much or too frequently amid the beautiful remains of the Caſtles and Abbeys of England.

Richard Barrett, Printer, 13, Mark Lane, London.

www.ingramcontent.com/pod-product-compliance
Lightning Source LLC
Chambersburg PA
CBHW031753230426
43669CB00007B/596